What people are saying about …

A Lifelong Love

"If you enjoyed the acclaimed and bestselling *Sacred Marriage* by Gary Thomas, you've got to read *A Lifelong Love*. This book is incredible. Consider it your road map to obtaining all that God designed your marriage to be. You absolutely don't want to miss out on this life-changing message."

Drs. Les and Leslie Parrott, authors of
Saving Your Marriage Before It Starts

"When Gary Thomas writes anything, I pay attention. When he writes about relationships or family, I pay more attention. When he writes about marriage, I pay attention in the fullest way possible. He has a rare gift to take what we may think we know, and turn it inside out for a fresh reexamination using Scripture. Marriage is the most important relationship we have apart from the one we have with God. I am thankful for Gary's passion and commitment to help us experience growth, no matter if we're newly married or married many years. This is yet another Gary Thomas book I will recommend and use both personally and as a pastor in our church."

Dan Kimball, pastor and author
of *Adventures in Churchland*

"*A Lifelong Love* is a powerful reminder that marriage is more than just a social construct or a legal arrangement. It is a deeply spiritual act ordained by God Himself. I believe married couples will find it practical and inspiring as they pursue deeper intimacy in their relationships."

Jim Daly, president of
Focus on the Family

"A profound, beautiful, and lifelong love in marriage is anchored in our relationship with God. This book takes you there!"

Dr. Tim Clinton, president of the American
Association of Christian Counselors

"Gary Thomas has done it again. *A Lifelong Love* is another timely, well-crafted book for every married couple. Gary's words carry some needed encouragement, instruction, and hope. This is not just another marriage book; it lifts marriage back to the noble place where it belongs ... one of transcendent and magnificent glory."

Dr. Dennis Rainey, host of
FamilyLife Today

"There are so many marriage books out there, but in my mind, Gary Thomas is like the *Good Housekeeping* Seal of Approval. I've thoroughly enjoyed so many of his works through the years, such as *Sacred Marriage* and *Pure Pleasure*, and I am thrilled that he's contributed yet another marriage-building, affair-proofing, family-strengthening, God-honoring book to guide those of us who take marriage very seriously!"

Shannon Ethridge, author of the bestselling Every Woman's Battle series and *The Passion Principles*

"Gary Thomas has written another deep and powerful book full of biblical wisdom and practical suggestions for a loving, lifelong marriage that is more than simply staying together, precisely because it is God-centered and empowered by the Holy Spirit. A must-read for every married couple!"

Siang-Yang Tan, professor of psychology at Fuller Theological Seminary and senior pastor of First Evangelical Church in Glendale, CA

"No other author I'm aware of offers such a spiritually rich framework for understanding and thriving in marriage. In *A Lifelong Love*, Gary Thomas powerfully cuts through all the hype to offer us real hope for a healthy marriage grounded in God. This is a deep, satisfying book that will lead you to the path of true joy in marriage."

Jud Wilhite, senior pastor of Central Christian Church and author of *Pursued*

"This book is like *Sacred Marriage* part two. Gary shows you how to practically live out your marriage with an eternal perspective. *A Lifelong Love* teaches the paradox of letting go of happiness and finding hope and mission in the process. Regardless of the state of your marriage, this book will challenge and encourage you!"

Dr. Juli Slattery, psychologist and
cofounder of Authentic Intimacy

"Many marriage books focus on skills, but this book builds skills on deep theology. I love Gary's reflective writing style. This book demands a sermon series, and our church will be one of the first to use it."

Ted Cunningham, pastor of Woodland Hills
Family Church and author of *Fun Loving You*

"In his newest book, Gary Thomas gives us the next steps on our journey to a sacred marriage. If you need a renewed sense of hope and purpose for your marriage, or simply long to become a couple that is more surrendered to God, devoted to one another, and engaged in the world, this book is for you! If you are a church family that wants to see marriages become more transformational and missional, then I would recommend every leader and spouse to go on the journey of *A Lifelong Love.*"

Dr. Michael Dittman, director
of Haven for the Heart

"Taking the broad topic of marriage and writing about it seems almost impossible, but God has gifted Gary Thomas to do such a thing at such a time as this! *A Lifelong Love* is deeply rooted in the Word of God as the ultimate guideline for marriage and is a must-read for everyone: married, thinking about it, single, or struggling in the marriage they are in. That's the answer to how to love your spouse well. Thank you once again, Gary, for a tremendous work!"

Cheryl Scruggs, Hope Matters
Marriage Ministries, Inc.

"If you are looking for an easy fix, sevens steps to perfect your spouse, or simple answers to complex marriage questions, *A Lifelong Love* is not the book for you. Gary Thomas builds on the brilliant and challenging message of *Sacred Marriage* as he helps us discover God's pathway to "a lifelong love." The journey will not always be easy, but it can be rich, alive with the presence of Jesus and more meaningful than we dream."

Kevin G. Harney, lead pastor of Shoreline
Community Church and author of
Empowered by His Presence and the Organic
Outreach series (www.kevingharney.com)

A LIFELONG LOVE

GARY THOMAS

A LIFELONG LOVE

How to Have Lasting Intimacy, Friendship,
and Purpose in Your Marriage

DAVID C COOK

transforming lives together

A LIFELONG LOVE
Published by David C Cook
4050 Lee Vance Drive
Colorado Springs, CO 80918 U.S.A.

Integrity Music Limited, a Division of David C Cook
Eastbourne, East Sussex BN23 6NT, England

The graphic circle C logo is a registered trademark of David C Cook.

The website addresses recommended throughout this book are offered as a
resource to you. These websites are not intended in any way to be or imply an
endorsement on the part of David C Cook, nor do we vouch for their content.

The author has changed some names and details of
testimonies in this book for the sake of privacy.

Unless otherwise noted, all Scripture quotations are taken from the Holy
Bible, New International Version®, NIV®. Copyright © 1973, 2011 by Biblica,
Inc.™ Used by permission of Zondervan. All rights reserved worldwide.
www.zondervan.com. Scripture quotations marked NASB are taken from the
New American Standard Bible®, Copyright © 1960, 1995 by The Lockman
Foundation. Used by permission. (www.Lockman.org); ESV are taken from The
Holy Bible, English Standard Version® (ESV®), copyright © 2001 by Crossway,
a publishing ministry of Good News Publishers. Used by permission. All
rights reserved; NLT are taken from the *Holy Bible*, New Living Translation,
copyright © 1996, 2007 by Tyndale House Foundation. Used by permission
of Tyndale House Publishers, Inc., Carol Stream, Illinois 60188. All rights
reserved; NRSV are taken from the New Revised Standard Version Bible,
copyright 1989, Division of Christian Education of the National Council of the
Churches of Christ in the United States of America. Used by permission. All
rights reserved; and ASV are taken from the American Standard Version. (Public
Domain.) The author has added italics to Scripture quotations for emphasis.

LCCN 2015936911
Hardcover ISBN 978-1-4347-0490-0
Paperback ISBN 978-1-4347-0862-5
eISBN 978-0-7814-1237-7

© 2014 Gary Thomas
Published in association with Yates & Yates, www.yates.com.

The Team: Alex Field, Karen Lee-Thorp, Jack Campbell,
Helen Macdonald, Amy Konyndyk, Karen Athen
Cover Design: Nick Lee

Printed in the United States of America
First Edition 2014

7 8 9 10 11 12 13 14 15 16

073018

*This book is dedicated in celebration of my son
Graham's marriage to Molly, on July 12, 2014.
May you both grow in grace and love for each
other as you enjoy the blessing of a lifelong love.*

Contents

Part Three: The Journey Toward Love

Acknowledgments

I am indebted to so many individuals who graciously gave their time, wisdom, and constructive comments in early drafts of this book: Karen Lee-Thorp (Karen is an extraordinary editor who, believe it or not, has read this manuscript at least five times in various incarnations, saving all of you from having to plow through a lot of fluff, repetition, and grammatical mistakes); Drs. Steve and Rebecca Wilke; Alfonso Gilbert; Dr. Melody Rhode; Mary Kay Smith; Mike Salisbury; Lisa Thomas; Dr. Gerrit Dawson; Dr. Mitch Whitman; Jeff and Cheryl Scruggs; Dr. Juli Slattery; Alli Smith; Toni Richmond; Brooks Powell; and John Stanley. I am further indebted to the congregation of Second Baptist Church, Houston, Texas (under the leadership of Dr. Ed Young and Ben Young), for their generosity in keeping me on as writer-in-residence.

I can't imagine writing without my agent, Curtis Yates. I am also very grateful for my friends at David C Cook—Alex Field, Dan Rich, Lisa Beech, Ingrid Beck, Helen Macdonald, Ginia Croker, Michael Covington, and others.

There is, of course, one person who could single-handedly torpedo or bless my life and ministry, and that's my wife of now thirty years (as of June 3, 2014), Lisa Thomas. She has lived this life and this truth with me, making it a delight and a joy to explore the reach of worship and intimacy in marriage. Lisa, thirty years ago, we began walking the journey of a lifelong love, and I'm still eager to see where it leads.

Introduction

I have loved you with an everlasting love; therefore I have drawn you
with lovingkindness. Again I will build you and you will be rebuilt.
—Jeremiah 31:3–4 NASB

It was an intentional slight, albeit an understandable one.

When German Mennonites started migrating to Belize in the 1950s, just a decade after the Nazis had thrown the entire world into chaos via World War II, Belizean officials were a bit wary. The Mennonites didn't look, act, or speak like Nazis, but they *were* Germans, so they were still suspect. What to do?

Here's an idea: give them the most unproductive land in the entire country, the property that no one else wants.

At least they can't wreck it. It's already wrecked!

For the sake of the country, and perhaps for the sake of the Mennonites, it was a brilliant decision, though not in the way the Belizean officials anticipated. By applying their faith and work ethic, the Mennonites eventually made their part of Belize not just productive and fruitful but, indeed, *the most fruitful and productive part of the entire country.* I was told that approximately 60 percent of Belize's most valuable natural resources now come from Mennonite-held lands—the property that, less than a hundred years ago, nobody else wanted.

"You know as soon as you hit the Mennonite area," a person from Belize once said to me. "You just know."

It's an inspiring tale, isn't it? The Belizean Mennonites, applying their faith, took the worst land in the country to work with and made it the most productive.

That's not a bad image for marriage. It is possible, with faith, to receive the least productive relationship and end up spiritually feeding others out of it. It is possible to enter marriage feeling as though you have nothing to give and end up having an incredibly fruitful relationship that isn't just fulfilling to you but inspiring to others. It is possible to feel as if you are stuck in a rut in your marriage—as if you and your spouse simply lack the "raw materials" or "natural resources" of compatibility and intimacy skills to ever achieve anything even resembling happiness in your marriage and yet, with faith, realize that marriage becomes a source of profound joy, rich togetherness, and powerful witness.

The spiritual principle is this: *it's not what we have; it's what we do with it.* When God becomes part of the equation, it's not what we get from or even bring into our marriages, but it's what we do with His empowering presence that creates a rich intimacy and a beautiful relationship.

Another way of looking at this is through the eyes of Booker T. Washington, the former slave who became such a surprising political force in the nineteenth century. Washington spoke of the "advantage of disadvantages." He believed that when difficulties called out your best, they became stepping-stones instead of roadblocks. They forced you to become stronger than you would otherwise have been.

The prophet Jeremiah proclaimed a bold promise from God to His people: "I have loved you with an everlasting love; therefore I have drawn you with lovingkindness. Again I will build you and you will be rebuilt" (Jer. 31:3–4 NASB).*

Time and time again, this passage has been proven to me in my marriage. When I understood how God had loved me with an everlasting love—that my marriage was first and foremost a magnificent obsession with God and His kingdom, above all things, even above my wife—my marriage changed radically for the good. I was drawn by and to His lovingkindness, as a recipient and then as an agent, seeking a much deeper expression of what it means to truly love, especially within marriage. This has been nothing short of revolutionary for me. And those two elements together—the magnificent obsession with God and the passion to pursue a deeper love—led into a third element, God building and rebuilding my marriage into

---

* I realize it is poor scriptural interpretation to take a promise to Israel and arbitrarily apply it to marriage; I am not intending to proof-text here but to use biblical language for a larger picture, each element of which *will* be supported with appropriately applied scriptures later in the text.

a more intimate union: "I will build you and you will be rebuilt." This puts hope for my marriage not just on a different plane or even planet but on a different existence altogether: *God* will do this.

These three elements form the base of a stool. Together, they provide a sturdy foundation to support us. If you take out just one—focusing on God and love but not intentionally growing together—you will be unbalanced and headed for a fall. If you focus on intimate union and love but not God, you will eventually lose your way.

The point of this approach is to acknowledge the triune God as the center, the model, and the empowering agent of my marriage. He sets the agenda for what I should desire, what I should strive for, and how I can get there. He even promises to make it happen: "I will build you and you will be rebuilt." This makes the meaning of my marriage something much bigger and grander than I ever could have dreamed. It's the journey beyond technique to worship, intimate union with my wife, and love.

This broad focus allows us to address virtually every season and condition of marriage: people who are frustrated with whom they married and who wonder how they can find fulfillment in the midst of it; those who believe they made generally good choices, but whose marriages haven't lived up to all they hoped they might be; and those who simply desire to take their marriages to new levels by bolstering them with a spiritual purpose and dynamic that has been lacking up till now.

Here's the question we seek to answer: How can we remake our marriages to become fruitful relationships that breathe spiritual life and that God can use to encourage others? My book *Sacred Marriage* gave a picture of the destination. This book is the road map of how to get there. *Sacred Marriage* spoke of the character God builds in us through marriage; *A Lifelong Love* addresses the intimacy that awaits us if we will lay hold of God's promises and spiritual provisions.

Let's begin with what I like to call the magnificent obsession.

Marriage Stool

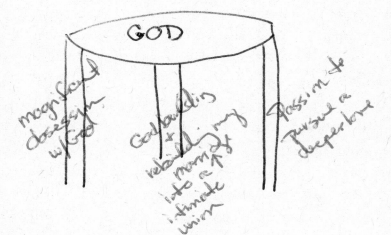

Part One

The Magnificent Obsession

1

The Magnificent Obsession

Marriage, designed by God, is a wonderful, fulfilling reality, a gift of God's grace, and a mark of His kindness because He allows us to know the joys of intimacy and family life. If I had a hundred lives to live, I'd want to be married in every one of them.

Yet marriage—even the best of marriages—is also a miserable substitute for the ultimate reality of living for God. Divorce rates testify that spouses who were once enthralled with each other—gripped by an infatuation so intense they could scarcely stand to be apart—eventually get bored with each other and now can't bear to live in the same house. Such shifts testify to the reality that none of us is so enthralling that we can keep someone enchanted for five or six decades. No one. Five or six dates? No problem. Five or six years? That's a challenge. Five or six decades? Good luck with that. So, it would seem natural to get a little bored with the same marital relationship.

Unless …

Unless we are "planted by streams of [spiritual] water" that keep our leaves from withering (Ps. 1:3). We need, I believe, a "magnificent obsession," an overriding purpose that ties our days together, gives comfort in the valleys, calls us forward in the suffering, highlights our joy in the springtime, and even seasons our ecstasies. That's what God provides in a marriage based on Him. This isn't some ethereal theory—it's very practical, and it can do more than merely hold our marriages together; it catapults them to new levels of fulfillment. In the end, selfishness is a very boring life.

In the first sermon he ever preached, the famous Puritan Jonathan Edwards dropped this brilliant passage: "The glorious excellencies and beauty of God will be what will forever entertain the minds of the saints, and the love of God will be their everlasting feast. The redeemed will indeed enjoy other things; they will enjoy the angels, and will enjoy one another: but that which they shall enjoy in the angels, or each other, or in anything else whatsoever that will yield them delight and happiness, will be what shall be seen of God in them."[1]

That last sentence is key: *That which they shall enjoy … will be what shall be seen of God in them.*

As God captures our hearts, we fall more and more in love with Him. He becomes all our desire, our very life and breath. There is a point in a mature believer's life when it would be impossible to truly revel in something that is in rebellion to God. The ancient classics talk about this all the time—the stages of soul formation in which we obey out of fear and then out of love, and then, because God has so captured our hearts, we obey because we only truly desire the good (that is, God). It's not that temptation can't seize such a soul—it surely can—but if we fall, we hate what we're doing even when we're doing it, and we're appalled by what we've done after it's over.

Which means that a marriage with a shared love of Christ—a magnificent obsession—is a marriage that grows ever deeper over time; as God shapes our hearts to desire Him, He is also, in that work, shaping our hearts to desire and enjoy each other. The more I love my wife out of worship, then the more God brings my heart into an ever-worshipful state (which He is doing steadily, continuously), and the more I will love my wife. I take delight in the eternal will of God, because God is giving me the heart to do so. His eternal will is that I love my wife as Christ loves the church, so I start to relish the thought and practice of loving my wife that way, because what I love in my marriage, what I love in my wife, is the presence of God.

What if your spouse isn't a believer? You can still enjoy the presence of God in your marriage because God's Word says, "The unbelieving husband has been sanctified through his wife, and the unbelieving wife has been sanctified through her believing husband" (1 Cor. 7:14). In this rather stunning statement, Paul boldly proclaims that there is enough of God in one believing spouse to provide everything a marriage needs to be sanctified.

God is that powerful.

What this means, friends, is that long-term marital satisfaction is found first and foremost in worship, in yielding our hearts first to God, and in cooperating with God's grace to make us not only do what is right but truly desire what is good and worthy of praise. The more we do that, the more we will cherish our spouses and our marriages, because we will never—not even in a million years—grow weary of Him. And He has so made us that we find our delight *only* in Him.

I don't care how rich your intimacy is, how thrilling and pleasurable your sexual life is, how successful your children are—these things alone cannot fill an otherwise empty soul for decades on end. You can have a good run with them, but they will not constitute a *lifelong* love. We were made to live with no less a drama than the spread of God's eternal reign. We *need* adventure. We *need* purpose. We *need* the adrenaline of stepping out of our comfort zones for a purpose higher than our own well-being. We *need* all of that, desperately, and we need it to matter for eternity, not just for the moment or for our bank accounts, our pleasure, or our reputations. It would be nice to live in a romantic comedy for ninety minutes or so, everything cute and funny, then wrapped up with a grand resolution, but wouldn't it be terribly boring to exist in a romantic comedy for ninety years?

Nothing else can substitute for kingdom life, because that's how God created us. Marriages without a magnificent obsession are racing toward boredom. It's only a matter of time.

So although relational intimacy, conversation, laughter, sex, and child raising may season our lives, these wonderful realities are not the end of life or the substance of life. It's not enough to simply raise a child—I need to raise a child because God desires godly offspring (Mal. 2:15). There's a purpose behind my child rearing.

In Christian circles, we do a disservice if we try to "fix" marriages without first proclaiming the necessity of fixing our lives on this magnificent obsession, the kingdom of God. I have no desire to offer five steps on how to be a little less miserable in your marriage as you live a substandard, selfish life that isn't set on the spread of God's work. But I will give plenty of time to help another believer jump into the current of God's advancing kingdom.

An influential man from an Asian country once invited me to speak in his city on behalf of the government. "The government will pay you very well," he promised, "and then you can speak to the churches for free."

I loved that model, until he added, "All you have to do, when speaking on behalf of the government, is to leave out the God stuff."

If I leave out the "God stuff," I've got nothing. What am I supposed to say? Compared to *Sacred Marriage*'s "What if God designed marriage to make us holy more than to make us happy,"[2] am I supposed to ask, "What if the government doesn't sanction marriage because it wants you to be happy but rather to be better citizens?" Sounds rather weak in comparison, don't you think?

To me, the only marriage I want is a marriage that is sacred through and through. Marriage provides me with a sister in Christ who walks with me as I serve God, and with whom I can grow in the ability to love. It gives me a holy outlet to enjoy and celebrate sexual pleasure. It provides a stable foundation from which I can raise children. It offers a glimpse to our neighbors of the relationship between Christ and the church. It provides the deepest friendship I have ever known. Marriage has been healing to me on many levels, but it is not my reason for being. To expect it to become that is to smother it. It would be like asking your baby, whom you love so much, to prepare your dinner. It's ludicrous and backward.

The best marriages are achieved by living for something else and letting that something else come back and lift up our marriages. The key to a happy marriage that becomes ever happier is a magnificent obsession outside of marriage.

In part 1, we're going to explore the "spiritual dimension" of marriage. How does our faith sustain, nurture, and focus our marriages?

Building a Lifelong Love

1. Do you agree that a lack of spiritual vitality helps to explain why so many (not all) couples start out so well and finish so poorly? Why or why not?
2. In your own marriage, how much has a shared pursuit and worship of God seasoned your relationship?

Our heavenly Father, You created us to find our highest pleasure in You. What we love most in others is what most reminds us of You. What gives us the power and desire to draw near to others is the very essence of Your own triune nature, one God existing in relationship. At the start of this journey, give us a new thirst to draw nearer to You, nearer to each other—regardless of any pain we've been through—and nearer to a more biblical expression of what it truly means to love. In Jesus's name, amen.

2

Worshipping Our Way to Happiness

Worship has long been a part of who I am; but my need for it, my desperate desire to live in it, seems to grow in intensity with every passing year. The more you worship, the more you want to worship. The more you glimpse God's world, the more you want to dwell there.

What this has meant for me is that the more I connect my marriage with worship, the more precious my marriage becomes. It is now on a rocket ship hurtling toward the heavens, leaving lesser motivations behind. If you will start to see your spouse as God sees your spouse, if you will cultivate the affection God already has for the person to whom you're married, your relationship will never be the same.

Let's establish the foundation by understanding who your spouse really is.

A Prayer That Left Me Gloriously Ruined*

It came almost as a warning, and frankly, I needed one at the time. I was a young husband, and during an intense time of prayer, I sensed God telling me very directly that Lisa wasn't just my wife, but she was also His daughter and I was to treat her accordingly. It was an intense application of 1 John 3:1: "See what kind of love the Father has given to us, that we should be called children of God" (ESV).

This was a moment of revelation for me, and the force of this insight grew once I had kids of my own. If you want to get on my good side, just be good to one of my kids. A wonderful young woman at our church became Allison's "big sister" when Ally was in her early teens, taking her out for coffee or ice cream and being an overall positive influence. My wife and I will love Amy for the rest of our lives for the way she was so generous to one of our children.

Conversely, if you really want to make me angry, pick on my kids. Be mean to them. My blood pressure will go up if your name is even mentioned because I'd much rather you mess with me than with one of my kids.

---

* Readers familiar with *Devotions for a Sacred Marriage* will note that I discuss this idea of God as Father-in-Law in that book as well. However, it's so central to how I believe we should view our marriages, and how (and why) we connect them to lives of worship, that I think it's essential to once again lay this foundation before moving on.

So when I realized I was married to *God's daughter*—and that you, women, were married to *God's sons*—everything about how I viewed marriage changed. God feels about my wife—His daughter—in an even holier and more passionate way than I feel about my own daughters. Suddenly, my marriage was no longer about just me and one other person; it was very much a relationship with a passionately interested third partner. I realized one of my primary forms of worship throughout the rest of my life would be honoring God by taking care of a woman who would always be, in His divine mind, "His little girl."

We often hear pastors contemplate the fatherhood of God, a wonderful and true doctrine. But if you want to change your marriage, extend this analogy and spend some time meditating about God as Father-*in-Law*. Because when you marry a believer, He is!

This is not to lessen the direct connection we have with God as our Father—something we should never compromise. No, it is not to lessen the depth of that connection but to help us married people widen the breadth of it. God is even more to us than a Father—He is also our Father-in-Law.

When I disrespect my wife or am condescending toward her or mistreat her in any way, I am courting trouble with her heavenly Father, who feels passionately about her welfare. "And remember that the heavenly Father to whom you pray has no favorites. He will judge or reward you according to what you do. So you must live in reverent fear of him during your time as 'foreigners in the land'" (1 Pet. 1:17 NLT). In a positive sense, when I am actively caring for my wife, loving her, and seeking opportunities to show-case her beauty to others, I am pleasing God on about as high a level as He can be pleased.

"She's Going to Be Okay"

My earthly father-in-law, Bill, had been battling leukemia for seven years. He was ready to go home with the Lord, and over the phone he literally asked me to pray that God would let him go home *that day*.

My mind went back to Lisa and our wedding rehearsal dinner, when Bill broke into tears telling me how happy he was about the next day's wedding. Bill wasn't particularly sentimental, and almost two decades passed before he explained what was behind the tears: "Gary, when you married my daughter, I thought to myself, *I don't have to worry about Lisa. She's found a guy who will take care of her. She's going to be okay.*"

Now that I have two daughters in their twenties, I can empathize. And so, during our last conversation, after mutually sharing some personal things, I told Bill, "I just want you to know how grateful I am that you gave me Lisa, and I want to remind you that you don't ever have to worry about Lisa. I'll make sure she's okay."

I said that because I could imagine that on my own deathbed, that would be exactly what I would want to hear. Secure about my eternal destiny (as Bill was about his), I'd be most concerned about those I was leaving behind. I'd want to know someone would be there for my daughters.

That day reminded me that the best gift I can give a father-in-law is to take care of and even spoil his little girl. Viewing God as Father-in-Law has helped me understand the apostle Peter's words when he wrote, "Husbands, in the same way be considerate as you live with your wives, and treat them with respect as the weaker partner and as heirs with you of the gracious gift of life, so that nothing will hinder your prayers" (1 Pet. 3:7).

That used to seem backward to me; I thought I needed to pray for a better marriage, but Peter is telling me I need a better marriage so I can pray. Looking at God through the lens of Father-in-Law resolved the dilemma. If a young man came to me, praising me, complimenting me on my character, even singing songs about me and giving me 10 percent of his income, and all the while I knew he was making one of my daughters miserable through abuse or neglect, I'd frankly have nothing to say to him except, "Hey, buddy, start treating my daughter better, and then we can talk. You say you respect me? Then take care of my little girl."

That would be the first and only thing I'd want to discuss with him every time he approached me. So it makes total sense to me that if I don't treat Lisa well, respecting her as God's daughter, with all the privileges such a high standing involves, my prayer life will be hindered.

A young woman, raised by a single mom, married into an extremely wealthy family. The family's wedding present to her was to pay off her considerable student loan and credit card debt, and *then they bought a house for her mom.* She wondered, "How can I ever repay them?"

My answer was simple: "Love their son as a husband has never been loved. There are few parents alive who wouldn't give most of what they have to see their children loved so well by their spouses."

I can never begin to repay God for what He has done for me. But I can love His daughter well. I can make Him smile by how I treat her. And one of His smiles is worth more to me than anything else in this world.

Imagine Your Son

Anna, a mother of five children all under eight years of age, is understandably tired. It's impossible *not* to be tired if you have five kids that young. She's married to Michael, a rising lawyer and almost-certain future partner of a prestigious law firm. The problem Anna wants resolved is a common one: Michael has a high sex drive, and Anna has almost none. She's understandably concerned that as Michael's star at work rises, particularly with younger associates and interns, he could be targeted for sexual temptation. But she's not concerned enough to have sex nearly as often as Michael would like.

"What do you think would make Michael happy?" I asked her.

"He told me he'd be happy with two times a week, ecstatic with three."

"As opposed to the current …"

"Maybe once a month, if I'm honest."

Once a month almost qualifies for a "sexless marriage." (An accepted definition by most marital therapists is ten times a year or less.)

There were extenuating circumstances that we talked about, and things I could and did say later to Michael, but the image that Anna later told me most opened her eyes was this: I asked her to imagine her oldest son all grown up, married, and with small kids. He works a busy job and travels through a pornographic world. His vocation requires him to be around young, energetic women, he's a star in their galaxy, and he also happens to have a high sex drive.

"Okaaaay …," Anna said.

"You want your son to be a faithful husband and a man of integrity, right?"

"Of course."

"And because you raised him right, he's doing his best. But I want you to consider this: If your future daughter-in-law treated him like you're treating Michael right now, would you be frustrated with her or grateful to her?"

Anna was silent for a long while, processing the question. Her voice dropped two levels of softness when she replied, "Well, I wouldn't be happy with her."

To get a feel for how well you're treating God's son, just consider how you'd feel if a daughter-in-law treated your boy the way you treat your husband, in any area. Would you thank God for her, or would you be pleading with God that He would convict her and soften her heart?

You see, worship of God as Father-in-Law helps keep our hearts soft and helps prevent us from the scourge of so many marriages: taking our spouses for granted. It also encourages us to stop being a "prosecuting attorney" and to start living as a "defense counselor."

From Prosecuting Attorney to Defense Counselor

The vicar (clergyman) in a small British village had heard enough. Jean had visited him once too often and always with the same complaint. The vicar's patience was at an end, so he exhorted Jean, "You've been coming here now for seven weeks. All I've been hearing is continual carping about how awful it has been for you being married to Reg, how mean and bad-tempered he is. I'm fed up with hearing the same old thing week in and week out. I don't want to hear any more. Before we go on, I want you to go into the church and ask God to show you just what life must have been like for Reg and why he's become as he is."

Jean found herself dumbfounded. "How could a man who called himself a priest be so unchristian and insensitive? Of course he was a man—men do stick together. He probably thought it was the woman's fault, as always!"

But then Jean went into the church to pray.

At first, she recited to God all the good things Reg had going for him—his meals cooked just the way he liked them, his clothes washed and even ironed, a sexually willing wife—what more could he want? What was his problem, God?

Once Jean's opinions ran out, God's thoughts crept in. God reminded Jean that two months after their wedding, Reg's partners in his advertising firm misspent company assets, forcing them out of business and Reg out of an income. Jean became disabled shortly thereafter and lost her job as well, leaving Reg and Jean all but homeless.

Then Reg's mother died, suddenly and unexpectedly. With little time or space to grieve, Reg had to find a place for his family to live, so they moved to Cornwall; but that didn't work out, forcing Reg to move his family back to his father's house in London.

Jean found herself speechless as this account rolled through her mind. She had been so full of words with the vicar—with God, not so much.

"As I sat there in that church, looking back into the past, it slowly dawned on me how all this must have affected Reg. His dreams had all been shattered in two short months—firm collapsed, mother dead, home gone—and he was back where he had started. He must have felt an utter failure. No wonder he seemed to turn against me and his son. He had to use us as a fuse or he would have blown his mind."

It's painful for me to copy that last sentence. No, Reg *didn't* have to use his family as a fuse, but let's allow Jean to finish her story, because that's the main point: "I'd never before thought about any situation from another person's viewpoint. I'd never experienced such hurt as I now began to feel on Reg's behalf—my own hurts, hates, and frustrations seemed nothing in comparison. Tears ran down my cheeks for him and all the unspoken feelings which he'd obviously had no idea how to cope with."[1]

Do you see what happened? In prayer, Jean's angry accusations transformed themselves into tears of empathy. She was no longer a prosecuting attorney; in prayer, she had become Reg's defense counselor.

This is the journey marriage calls us to, to seek to understand and empathize, for each of us to strive to become a redemptive partner rather than a legal opponent. If we truly want to love God's sons and daughters, we have to seek to understand God's sons and daughters. *Men and women, have you ever asked God why your spouses are the way they are?* In the midst of your frustration, have you ever sought God's perspective for what has "bent" them in their current direction?

We must be for our spouses as God is for us (see Rom. 8:31), as God was for us even in our sins. Do you realize that in the height of your rebellion against God, He was for you? That He was working out your plan of salvation, softening your heart, calling you into His kingdom? You never somehow found goodness within you and released it to the point where God had to forgive you. In your deepest rebellion and most selfish state, God called you out of the darkness into His wonderful light.

That's how God treated you. So is it too much for Him to ask us to treat our spouses—His sons and daughters—with the same grace we have received?

Evil in a spouse can't be excused, but it can be understood. I don't want any wife to try to "explain away" abusive behavior. Please don't take this the wrong way. But marriage does call us to at least try to understand our spouses' struggles as God understands them—looking through the kindly, paternal eyes of our loving heavenly Father-in-Law instead of through our angry, resentful eyes of judgment.

We can have empathy for others even while despising what they are doing. We can completely disagree with their *responses* even as we feel for their *pain*.

That's the key—our relationship with God means He never loses His empathy for His children, even as He truly hates when we sin or hurt others. We must not lose our empathy either, especially for our spouses. When we go into prayer as Jean went into prayer, if we will listen, God can help us see the "other side"—that is, the burdens and hurts of our spouses—instead of being consumed by *our* burdens and hurts.

Try this: Set some time aside in the next few days. If you have to spill out your frustrations and accusations to clear your mind, have at it. God is big enough to handle it. But stay on your knees long enough for God to wait until you're finished, and then listen as He redirects your thoughts to see your spouse's life as He has seen it—the hurts, the struggles, the disappointments, the heartaches. This doesn't mean your spouse's actions will be exempt from consequences, but it does mean you will feel differently about those consequences and let them unfold with an entirely different motivation—a holy one.

May God so transform us that we learn to respond to evil with holy hearts.

Imperfect Kids Are Still Kids

One summer, just before my son left for his first year of college, I kiddingly told him that I could write down the first three arguments he'd have with his future wife. I knew him that well, and I knew exactly where there was likely to be tension between him and a wife. At the time, he didn't even have a girlfriend, but when he did get one, their first disagreement was on that list.

And yet, though I know where he is likely to fail, though I am also fully aware of where my daughters are weakest and most likely to try their spouses' patience, it's almost scary to me how desperately I want them to be loved. There are three people on this earth who could make me among the happiest of men, simply by loving my children in an extraordinary way. I want my son to find a woman who will honor, respect, and support him even in the midst of his weaknesses and sins. I want each of my daughters to find a man who will still adore her, love her, and make her feel safe and secure, even though at times they can wake up with an attitude. None of my kids is perfect, but they'll always be my kids, which is why I'll always love the people who love them.

It is no different with our heavenly Father-in-Law. In the book of Jeremiah, God proclaims how eager He is to take even His rebellious children back: "'Is Ephraim My dear son? Is he a delightful child? Indeed, as often as I have spoken against him, I certainly still remember him; therefore My heart yearns for him; I will surely have mercy on him,' declares the LORD" (31:20 NASB).

God is fully aware of our spouses' limitations—and He is just as eager for us to be kind and generous with these faults as we are for our kids' future spouses to be kind to them when they stumble.

Women, if you married your man and dreamed of long, soul-filled discussions late into the night but six months after the wedding realized you married a man who wouldn't know an emotion if it bit him on the nose until he bled, process your frustration with the understanding that you made a good God very happy by agreeing to love His son with all his limitations. Picture my earthly father-in-law crying at the rehearsal dinner, overcome with emotion because he thought his child was now secure in her husband's love, and you'll get a dim but compelling picture of how your heavenly Father rejoiced when your spouse made the decision to marry *you*. Your disappointment at perhaps not having the marriage you imagined is understandable, but your worship toward God by loving your husband anyway is a precious thing that will be richly rewarded in eternity *and* will greatly impact your life on earth as well.

Men, if you married your woman not realizing that breast cancer or Alzheimer's was in her future, and you want to say to yourself, "I didn't sign up for this!" consider also how much joy you gave to your heavenly Father-in-Law when He could say, on the day you got married, "I'm so pleased Julie (or Katherine or Danielle) is with a good man who will stay with her and care for her out of reverence for Me. I know what's in her future, and I'll give this man what he needs; I just want him to take care of My little girl."

One of the things I love about this is that "secular" love is based on things that constantly change: health, beauty, mutual enjoyment of each other, and circumstance. My wife will *never* stop being God's daughter, so my main reason for loving her will never change. If she is an eighty-year-old arthritic Alzheimer's patient, she will be no less God's daughter than she is now. And I must never mistreat her, demean her, or do anything to dishonor her any more than I'd want my own daughter to be demeaned or cheated on.

What if I ran all my actions through this grid: "If my son-in-law treated my daughter the way I'm treating my wife, how would I feel?"

Men, that's the way what you're doing looks like to God. Women, just switch the genders. Imagine hearing your (perhaps future) daughter-in-law talking to her friends about your son with the same tone and words you use to describe your husband: How does that feel?

Things become so much clearer and evil becomes so much more transparent when we look at what we're doing through the eyes of a benevolent parent instead of an aggrieved spouse.

I want to be a faithful son-in-law, one who makes God proud, one who makes God smile, one who makes God sigh with satisfaction when He watches how I care for and treat my wife, His daughter.

With such an attitude, marriage becomes a central part of our worship. We learn to love imperfect people by serving them out of reverence for a perfect God, who loved us in the midst of our own brokenness. "We love because he first loved us" (1 John 4:19).

We all owe God more than we could ever know. He not only created us, but He redeemed us as well. He continues to forgive us. He teaches us. He encourages us. He protects us (in ways we don't even know about). He provides us with a reason to live. His wisdom is beyond wonderful. His acceptance is the basis for our ability to face our shame. When I owe someone so much, He can ask of me anything He wants. I am magnificently obsessed with this God, and one of the things He wants most particularly is for me to take care of His little girl.

Even if you spent ten years thinking about it, you'd still fall far short of understanding just how much God truly cares about your spouse. The Bible describes our believing spouses not just as children but also as "*dearly loved* children" (Eph. 5:1). A good bit of their comfort, happiness, and care is in our hands. What are we going to do with that?

Let's not just seek to avoid grieving Him, however; let's seek to make God clap.

Making God Clap

I spoke at a high school football banquet one time. High school is that age when some males still look like boys and others look like men. Some carry themselves with the grace, authority, and confidence of a CEO; others look like a puppy afraid of its own tail, just waiting to be hit.

But when these boys get their names called to receive their awards, everyone finds out where their parents are sitting. The clapping is a little too loud; often, the verbal comments are raucous. The family table erupts.

Why? Because parents love to see their children get recognized and honored.

If only we could see that God feels the same way. Oh, how He longs to honor the sons or daughters we are married to; how He delights in those who sing our spouses' praises.

If only we could see that it's not enough to refrain from despising. Christian marriage—sacred marriage—isn't simply about avoiding mockery or abuse. It's not about "not doing" what non-Christian spouses do. Sacred marriage is about so much more: if we could only see how much God wants us to honor our spouses in the eyes of others, in the eyes of heaven, in private and alone.

You know what I found particularly interesting at the banquet? The clapping the MVP award winner received from his family was not any louder than the clapping for the meekest, most out-of-shape-looking kid, who walked up to the stage with downcast eyes, almost missing the coach's handshake (literally!). That's because that meek-looking kid belonged to his parents. They didn't care whether he was the best, the bravest, the most improved, or the "iron man." You know what they cared about? He was *theirs*. He belonged to them, and he was being honored. That's what made them clap and cheer when his name was called.

Your spouse may not be the MVP. She may not win the bravery award, or he may not win the coaches' award. But your spouse is God's son or God's daughter. And God claps when He sees one of His kids honored.

Let's make God clap today. Let's honor His sons and daughters—the ones we're married to.

Building a Lifelong Love

1. Write down at least ten things God has done for you for which you are eternally grateful; praise Him for the way He has loved

you, the very fact that you exist, His kindness in calling you to faith, and so on.

2. If you have kids (if you don't, imagine that you do), write down three things that you particularly hope your future sons- or daughters-in-law will be or do consistently in their marriages to your children. Are you doing those things to God's son or daughter?

3. Why do you think your spouse is the way he or she is? Review your husband's or wife's history and determine what has been his or her greatest wound, relationally. What is his or her biggest disappointment? What insecurities do you think he or she might be trying to mask?

4. What is the fine line between understanding why our spouses are the way they are without excusing their behavior? Parents love their kids but still discipline and confront them; how does the same benevolence affect the way we address our spouses' sins within marriage?

5. What is one way you can make God clap today by honoring His daughter or son?

Our heavenly Father-in-Law, we boldly pray for Your revelation to help us better understand just how passionately You care about us both, Your son and Your daughter. Let us see each other with fresh eyes. Remind us of Your goodness, the goodness we so often take for granted, and out of that gratitude build in us a new determination to love as we have been loved. Whenever we approach You in worship or prayer, make us newly sensitive to one of the best ways we can bring You joy—taking care of Your son and daughter. In Jesus's name, amen.

3

Making the Last Things the First Thing Today

Do you know why the Pilgrims called themselves "pilgrims"?

It's not because they were pilgrims from Europe coming to the United States; their view of being pilgrims was much bigger than that. They called themselves pilgrims because, according to William Bradford (their first leader), they recognized this world (in its present state) was not their home. "For here we do not have a lasting city, but we are seeking the city which is to come" (Heb. 13:14 NASB). They weren't pilgrims because they had left Europe; they were pilgrims because they were still on earth, awaiting heaven that is to come.

The vast majority of marriage books take a decidedly short-term view. One man, who's written many books I have greatly enjoyed, even wrote about having "a new husband" by the weekend.

I get this. We want to know how we can fix our marriages today. The thought that there could be a significant difference in our marriages right away can be a compelling reason to shell out the money for a book.

Which is why I have been warned not to include a chapter like this, and certainly not so near the beginning. One polling organization even warned teachers that we completely lose the younger generation when we begin to speak of heaven and the afterlife.

The reason I'm willing to take a risk is because I have become more convinced, not less, about how crucial an eternal perspective is in order to make sense of marriage in the here and now. If I want to love my wife with an excelling love, a God-honoring love, if I want to plumb the depths of what marriage really means and understand the glory behind this earthly relationship, I have to remember that I am a pilgrim here. If you're younger, will you please prove the prognosticators wrong and give me your attention while I try to make precisely this case?

Well Done

The pilgrims lived, as we should live, with this glorious truth in mind: "For we must all appear before the judgment seat of Christ, so that each of us may receive what is due us for the things done while in the body, whether good or bad" (2 Cor. 5:10).

What Paul is referring to here is called the "judgment seat of Christ," a day that every Christian will face at the dawn of eternity. This is not a judgment of whether or not we will spend eternity with God—that is safe and secure in the finished work of Jesus on the cross and refers to a different judgment altogether.

The judgment seat of Christ is rather a proclamation of what we have done with God's grace and provision in our lives. That phrase "whether good or bad" could just as well be translated "whether good or worthless." (There's a different word Paul could have chosen if he had wanted to pinpoint "evil.") We will be asked, Did we respond to the powerful cleansing of God's mercy by sitting on our hands and soaking up God's blessings while filling our days with worthless pursuits and selfish preoccupations? Or did we, like Paul, work with the understanding that we must give an account of our days to our heavenly Father?

It's not about getting into heaven as much as what is offered to us within heaven. Our eternity will be stamped by the judgment made on that day, and the judgment made on that day will be rendered by how we live these days on earth.

Paul built on this in Romans 2, proving that this was a central theme in his teaching (and thus, God's revelation) to the early church: "He will render to each one according to his works: to those who by patience in well-doing seek for glory and honor and immortality, he will give eternal life; but for those who are self-seeking and do not obey the truth, but obey unrighteousness, there will be wrath and fury…. For God shows no partiality" (vv. 6–8, 11 ESV).

There is no shame in seeking glory and honor, only in seeking glory and honor *in the wrong time and from the wrong person*.

What Jonathan Edwards, the last of the great Puritans, said in the eighteenth century agrees with what virtually all the Christian classics have said for two thousand years, though this teaching has been severely deemphasized in the current generation: "This life ought to be so spent by us, as to be only a journey or pilgrimage towards heaven."[1]

Most of us look at how to make our marriages more pleasant or more fulfilling right now. Scripture urges us to set our sights much higher—how we live our marriages here can affect us in eternity for eternity.

It's not just Edwards's opinion—what he and so many writers are reacting to are the verses in Hebrews 11 that list many heroic saints who never received everything they were promised, but they admitted "that they were foreigners and strangers on earth. People who say such things show that they are looking for a country of their own.... They were longing for a better country—a heavenly one. Therefore God is not ashamed to be called their God, for he has prepared a city for them" (vv. 13–14, 16).

Do we, as we are called to do, live this life preparing for the new heavens and the new earth (Rev. 21:1)? Or do we insist, in marriage and all our relationships, that God make everything right this week, this month, or at least this year? If we are kind in our marriages, we expect to eat the fruit of that kindness within minutes. We have little sense of patient endurance, loving without earthly reward while waiting for God to set all things right in the end. We want "a new husband" this weekend! We want "a new wife" with one sermon! We've put in the effort—shouldn't those efforts be rewarded?

Well, yes—but not necessarily on this earth.

When I live for rewards in this life, when I seek primary happiness in the here and now, I'm discounting all the promises of God about what's to come. Now, certainly, living a godly life produces many rewards in this life. We rightfully celebrate those rewards and are thankful for those blessings. But God has told us He is preparing an even better place; He has said that while there are many blessings on this good earth that we can receive with thanksgiving, our ultimate reward won't be found here. Ultimate happiness and fulfillment won't be found here. They are waiting for us in the new heavens and the new earth, so at the very least, let's live our lives *here* remembering the importance of preparing for life *there*.

To forget about the new heavens and the new earth is to lose sight of the solid point of reference that keeps us headed in the right direction. Because God is such a good Creator, earthly delights such as laughter, friendship, good meals, art, sex, and conversation can almost tempt us to think, *Life doesn't get any better than this.* But God says it does. Very much so!

Here's Edwards's take:

> Though surrounded with outward enjoyments, and settled in families with desirable friends and relations; though we have companions whose society is delightful, and children in whom we see many promising qualifications; though we live by good neighbors, and are generally beloved where known, yet we ought not to take our rest in these things as our portion.

We should be so far from resting in them, that
we should desire to leave them all, in God's due
time. We ought to possess, enjoy, and use them,
with no other view but readily to quit them,
whenever we are called to it, and to change
them willingly and cheerfully for heaven.[2]

Edwards then added that we should "desire heaven more than
the comforts and enjoyments of this life."

All of these lesser things constitute a good obsession, but they
are not a magnificent obsession. Are we living as "foreigners and
strangers" or as citizens of this earth? Have we forgotten that we
are visitors?

Do I have a problem with good meals, wonderful social times,
pride in children, and the ecstasies of sexual intimacy? Of course
not! Thank God we can enjoy His many blessings with gratitude
and even worship. The two realities needn't be at war with each
other; one could even say that the temporal blessings can point to
and remind us of eternal blessings.

If, however, we start enjoying these things in an attitude of
forgetfulness about where we're traveling to and what we're living for,
we'll lack the power, the will, and the perspective to make eternally
profitable choices when we don't experience immediate payoffs.
(What rewards of intimate conversation await a spouse caring for
a husband or wife in the advanced stages of Alzheimer's?) When
you love your spouse but are spurned in return, when you give
sacrificially and are not even thanked, when you stay committed

and are "rewarded" with a spouse's apathy or even infidelity, does that mean God's words aren't true? Does that mean God isn't powerful enough to save?

A woman once asked me, "What happens when a sacred marriage doesn't work?" My response to this type of question is simple: just because a sacred marriage hasn't produced desired change in your spouse doesn't mean it hasn't "worked," provided it's produced desired change in you. God has promised to set things right, and He will. But He reserves the right to do so on a calendar of His choosing, not ours—even if it means after our deaths. This can provide great endurance for those of you who are disappointed in this life, who feel as though you give and give and give and don't reap the response from your spouse that many popular marriage books promise you.

If we are living for life in the new heavens and the new earth, the spiritual riches that await us will help us maintain proper spiritual priorities.

- We will choose the path of holiness over the path of what brings us the most immediate pleasure.
- We will choose the path of obedience over the path of ease.
- We will choose the path of stewardship over the path of self-indulgence.
- We will choose the path of diligence over the path of lost focus.

When I drove my daughter's car from Houston to Portland, Oregon (in anticipation of her move), I made progress every day. I didn't get lost in Colorado Springs; I didn't buy a home in Rawlins, Wyoming. I passed right through Ogden, Utah. I wanted to make progress every day, because I knew there was a destination (Portland) that I had to reach. The radical teaching of an eternal perspective is that all of us need to view this life as a journey, not as a final destination; otherwise, we'll make some very poor choices. If you're wandering in your faith, if you're less than diligent, you've likely forgotten about the final destination. You're not living with a magnificent obsession.

This is not to suggest we shouldn't plan or enjoy good meals, rich social times, vacations, date nights, and the like. When I'm traveling, I'll occasionally stop and go out of my way to be refreshed. We can thank God that He offers us many wonderful times on this earth. An Olympic athlete in training will go to the movies, read a book, stroll through a museum, and have dinner out with friends. But she will never forget she's in training, and she won't do anything that will undercut her training. Not if she's serious about winning a gold medal. She certainly wouldn't tire herself out trying to win the Safeway 5K race in Paris, Texas, the day before she runs in the Olympic trials. She gives up focusing on the lesser so she can save her best efforts, and express her most earnest passion, for the greater.

Ask yourself: In my marriage, how often do I get trapped into fighting over things that, in the end, don't really matter? How many marital problems would be solved if couples would simply read the Sermon on the Mount (Matt. 5–7) once a month, together?

This isn't to disdain the things of the earth—no need to do that—it's to exalt the things of heaven. Edwards wrote like a poet: "Fathers and mothers, husbands, wives or children, or the company of earthly friends, are but shadows; but the enjoyment of God is the substance. These are but scattered beams, but God is the sun. These are but streams; but God is the fountain. These are but drops, but God is the ocean."[3]

These are but drops, but God is the ocean.

All of this means we have to work at keeping our focus, our magnificent obsession; otherwise, we might put all our focus on lesser (but still important) aims—trying to improve our communication, get our finances in order, keep our romance fresh and fun, and so on. We have to remember that these are not the stuff of life and they are not the end goal. After all, as Edwards reminds us, "If our lives be not a journey towards heaven, they will be a journey to hell."[4]

If you truly desire to live as a pilgrim, gather with some good friends on a monthly basis and ask one another: "How is the hope of heaven influencing the way we love one another, the way we raise our kids, the way we spend our money, and the way we focus our time?"

Now, what I'm about to say may sound flat-out bizarre to some of you, but hang with me. If I want to love my wife with a biblical passion and biblical priorities, even more than I want her to have many happy birthdays, I will seek to help her have a supremely happy death day.

Happy Death Day

Precious in the sight of the LORD is the death of His godly ones.
—Psalm 116:15 NASB

What kind of God looks forward to His kids dying? The answer is the kind of God who knows what heavenly treasures await them.

The Bible presents God almost as if He is an eager parent on Christmas Eve, excited to lavish His children with gifts the next morning. He's excited about our judgment day because He knows our sins are covered by the finished work of Christ, and now He can greet us with the gifts He has been preparing for us.

This might offend some of you, but Jesus doesn't talk of equality in heaven; He speaks of those who are greater or lesser in the kingdom (Matt. 5:19) and of those who will receive great rewards or lesser rewards (Matt. 5:12). In a similar, negative way, some in hell will be "beaten with many blows," while others will be "beaten with few blows" (Luke 12:47–48).

As Jesus calls His disciples to a higher way of living, He freely uses reward terminology to motivate them: "Store up for yourselves treasures in heaven" (Matt. 6:20; cf. 6:4; 6:6; 6:18).

The writer of Hebrews stresses that not accepting the reality of heavenly rewards has dire consequences for our faith, because "anyone who comes to [God] must believe that he exists *and that he rewards those who earnestly seek him*" (Heb. 11:6). Paul backs this up in Ephesians 6:8: "The Lord will reward each one for whatever good they do."

Now, we don't know the full substance of all these rewards. We can know, with some certainty, it is not about seventy virgins. Please, God, no! What we can do is rest in the certainty that God knows what kinds of rewards are most appropriate and meaningful. God's silence on this issue might be similar to a father not wanting to spoil a Christmas morning surprise.

That Conversation on *That* Day

Notice that Paul said the Lord will reward us for "whatever good we *do*," not whatever good we *receive*.* This understanding alone can radically revolutionize the way we face each day of marriage.

On the day that theologians call the judgment seat of Christ, God will have a conversation with each one of us. In the course of that conversation, we will look at what happened to us—including within our marriages—from an entirely different perspective, one that is virtually opposite from how most of us view our marriages today. I will be rewarded, not for how my wife loved me, but for how I loved my wife (God's daughter). God won't ask, "Gary, did Lisa know your love language and honor it? Did she understand that you need respect and respect you? Did she have sexual relations

---

* Paul is *not* denying that *salvation* is *entirely* based on what we receive—grace flowing out of the substitutionary atonement of Christ. He's speaking of a different reality here—rewards, not salvation.

with you as often as you wanted? Did she know your needs and strive to meet them?"

Instead, He will ask—and my eternity will be stamped by my answers—"Gary, did you know Lisa's love language and were you generous with that knowledge? Did you understand her need for affection and acceptance and love and lavish her with that? Did you make the bedroom a place of blessing and mutual service? Did you seek to help her become all that I created her to be, or did you treat her as a servant designed to fulfill your own needs and desires?"

If I am living for today, a "good day" is when Lisa notices me, appreciates me, serves me, and makes my life more enjoyable. I lived for years in my marriage with that as my definition of a "good day." Living for eternity, a "good day" is when I notice Lisa, appreciate Lisa, serve Lisa, and make her life more enjoyable, because *that's* what will be rewarded at the judgment seat of Christ.

Consider the radical words of Jesus Christ in Luke 6:32–35, when He describes what it means to love, and notice the promise of rewards as motivation:

> If you love those who love you, what benefit is that to you? For even sinners love those who love them. And if you do good to those who do good to you, what benefit is that to you? For even sinners do the same. And if you lend to those from whom you expect to receive, what credit is that to you? Even sinners lend to sinners, to get

back the same amount. But love your enemies, and do good, and lend, expecting nothing in return, and your reward will be great, and you will be sons of the Most High, for he is kind to the ungrateful and the evil. (ESV)

Our reward will be great, Jesus said, not when we love people who love us back, but when we love "the ungrateful and the evil" as God does.

If you are married to the godliest, kindest, most giving and thoughtful spouse who ever lived, *that* will be your reward. There will be no extra credit in the heavenlies for having enjoyed an easier marriage than most. So you'll have some very pleasant decades, while someone else may be storing up for eternity.

If, for instance, your spouse takes you for granted, you may never be appreciated *on this earth*, but the day will come—Jesus promises it!—when you see your heavenly Father-in-Law face-to-face and He says to you, "You loved My son (or daughter) so well, even though I know he never understood how blessed he was to be married to you. Now, let Me show you how I spend all of eternity rewarding those who love in My name. Receive your rewards, enter into your rest!"

You see how believing in *that* day changes how we define what is a good day on *this* day? We'll look for opportunities to love, serve, notice, encourage, and appreciate, instead of being obsessed with how well our spouses are loving, serving, noticing, encouraging, and appreciating us. This is encouraging for those of you who are taken for granted. Let's be honest: some of you married fools. I don't mean to be flippant, but the Bible says there are fools, right? It seems to me, somebody must marry them. Maybe you picked one. From an earthly perspective, that's a wasted life. From an eternal perspective, you have the opportunity to set yourself up for a particularly thrilling and fulfilling "death day" conversation at the judgment seat of Christ.

Your spouse may never thank you, but you'll find an eager heavenly Father-in-Law who will tell you He didn't miss a single act of service and He has been eagerly waiting for your death day to arrive so that He can reward you for your love.

This is a truth that creates endurance and perspective. Consider the words of the apostle Paul in 2 Corinthians 4:16–18: "Therefore we do not lose heart. Though outwardly we are wasting away, yet inwardly we are being renewed day by day. For our light and momentary troubles are achieving for us an eternal glory that far outweighs them all. So we fix our eyes not on what is seen, but on what is unseen, since what is seen is temporary, but what is unseen is eternal."

In the book of Colossians, Paul even directly connected judgment rewards with marriage and family life. He told wives to treat their husbands "as is fitting in the Lord" (3:18); husbands to love their wives and never be harsh with them (v. 19); and then explained, "Whatever you do, work at it with all your heart, as working for the Lord, … since you know that you will receive an inheritance from the Lord as a reward. It is the Lord Christ you are serving" (vv. 23–24).

Mutual Partnership

Those of you who married godly spouses might be thinking, *Will I miss out? I have such a wonderful spouse who is relatively easy to live with. How will I get any heavenly rewards?*

Marriage isn't by any means the only pathway to eternal blessing. Far from it. Jesus was never married and will be celebrated above all. John the Baptist, the apostle Paul (at least postconversion), and many others will be celebrated not for what they did in marriage but for their faithfulness as singles.

Happily married couples who will embrace the judgment day of Christ as setting their agenda for today can take Hebrews 10:24 as their theme verse: "Let us consider how to stimulate one another to love and good deeds" (NASB).

If God rewards acts of love and good deeds, how can we encourage each other, pray for each other, and stimulate each other to do good deeds?

Again, lest I be misunderstood, this is *not* about salvation. This is *not* about gaining God's ultimate acceptance. That is settled by the death and resurrection of Christ. But there are so many passages where Christians are urged to be rich in good deeds, and a good marriage will seek to inspire each partner to store up these heavenly rewards.

What better gift could I give my wife than to help her do something for which she will be rewarded in heaven? What if I prayed for her, suggested something to her, supported her, and encouraged her so that she became more than she ever would have been as a single woman? Not only will she receive the blessing of obedience in this life, but I will also have literally set her up for multiple blessings in the next life. What a tremendous gift!

So you see, living for *that day* is not some religious form of avoidance. It's not about checking out of this earth. It's about checking into the earth with a new intensity and focus as God's redeeming work reveals itself through us and sets us up for eternal rewards.

Remember: on that day, we won't be asked how well we were loved; we'll be asked, "How well did *you* love?"

The Last Day of Marriage

Jesus's famous words at the end of the crucifixion, "It is finished," declare with glorious finality the completion of a passionate mission. In just three words, Jesus proclaimed that He had lived a supremely obedient, meaningful, and triumphant life.

There will come a time when each of us is also minutes away from death's door. As married people, one of our promises to God was to love His son or daughter like he or she has never been loved by any other human. We men pledged to be our wives' living martyrs (Eph. 5:25–26); you women were even urged to undergo training to learn how to love your husbands (Titus 2:4)—you were called to take your marriage so seriously that you felt you needed to be trained for it. These are sobering passages, leading us to much reflection, diligent practice, and unending prayer and counsel. And since we marry people who "stumble in many ways"

(James 3:2), these are not easy commitments to keep. There will be some seasons when it feels difficult, perhaps even impossible, to love like this.

But there is a finish line! There will be a day when the race is over, when it all comes to an earthly end. And our goal for that day is given to us here from Jesus's own mouth: "It is finished."

This is definitely *not* to suggest that marriage is gritting our teeth and hanging in there until the personal trainer blows his whistle and tells us the plank session is over and we can finally relax. It's more like loving each other as best we can—even if that means nursing an Alzheimer's patient or being faithful to a some-times-distracted spouse—until the present earthly limitations are peeled away and we can build on the love we have shared for fifty to seventy years. Though we won't be married in eternity, we will still be intimate in eternity, and will be able to know each other and be known even more deeply with even more joy.

That spouse who has momentarily forgotten who you are will finally be able to say, "You were so, so kind to me!" That spouse whose moral lapses tried your patience to the breaking point, now glorified, will likely extol your love by saying, "I can't believe you put up with me!" Your spouse who has been your best friend, with whom there were many seasons of laughter and, relatively speaking, not that many tears, will simply smile and say, "It was a good life, wasn't it? And who would have known that it could get so much better, to this degree? I never thought I could love you more than I did then, but now you are even more beautiful to me."

Think forward to the day when you will see your spouse's body laid to rest, or you yourself will be the one lying on your deathbed, waiting for your soul to be passed from this life to the next. Will you be able to say, as Jesus said, with some finality, "It is finished"?

"I loved her with passion, drawing upon God's power every day, until the very end."

"We not only survived our marriage, we thrived. Today is a day to celebrate what we accomplished in life together."

"I spent so much time in our marriage to lead him closer to the Lord, and now he is finally there. While I'll miss him terribly until we are reunited, I couldn't be happier for the journey we accomplished."

There is a day, friends, when this marriage stuff will come to an end, a day when God will look at how we have loved His sons or His daughters, and we will be judged accordingly. For some of you, that will lead to many eternal rewards. God is not stingy when it comes to rewarding those who faithfully serve His children.

Building a Lifelong Love

1. Was the idea of the judgment seat of Christ unfamiliar to you? How can understanding this teaching keep us focused in our love? Persevering in our love?

2. Is it wrong to want to improve our marriages on this earth? How do we keep this teaching about the judgment seat of Christ in perspective?

3. How did you previously define a "good day in marriage"? How would you define a good day now and into the future?

4. Many Christians define holiness as not doing a lot of things—not saying certain words, not stealing, not being sexually promiscuous, and so forth. How does the judgment seat of Christ transform us toward a positive view of holiness—Jesus's and Paul's admonitions to do good works?

5. How can you and your spouse fulfill the teaching in Hebrews and stimulate each other toward good works?

6. Think about your last day of marriage—how do you want to look back on your relationship, on how well you have loved your spouse? What can you begin doing today to help make that happen?

Our eternal Father, You have made such a wonderful world that, even in its fallen state, we can be lulled to sleep, forgetting that we are but pilgrims. Help us to remember where our true citizenship resides. Let us stop seeking to receive our rewards here and by faith patiently wait to receive our eternal rewards from You. Let us define a "good day" in marriage by faith—knowing that if there is an opportunity to notice, to encourage, to serve, that is a very good day in the eyes of eternity. We pray that we would not forget there is a last day of marriage on this earth and that we would live accordingly this day. In Jesus's name, amen.

4

The Glory of
Spiritual Dependence

Of all the things that Jesus did that showed His faith in the power
and sufficiency of the Trinity, dying so young was among the most
telling. Think about it: How much more could Jesus, God in flesh,
have done on this earth if He had given Himself another thirty years
of active, incarnational ministry rather than three? It's stunning
to consider: He could have performed many more healings and
miracles so that the church would number in the hundreds of thou-
sands rather than the few hundred who believed at His death. He
could have written dozens of books rather than relying on inspired
earthly intermediaries like Matthew, Paul, John, and Peter (there
would have been no questions about which books were authorita-
tive then). He could have established churches, putting the leaders
in place under His authority so that no one would question them,
and then we'd finally have the definitive answer to proper church

structure, leadership, and practice that the church has debated for more than two thousand years.

Why did Jesus leave so soon? Why did He leave the church so seemingly unprepared?

The answer is clear: He didn't, not really. Jesus had great confidence in the Holy Spirit. He told His disciples that this comforter and counselor would lead them to do even greater things than He had done and so He could leave with full confidence that even in His physical absence, all that would need to be done would be done.

Do we live with this confidence in the Holy Spirit for our lives, our marriages, and our families? Let's learn to trust the Holy Spirit, as Jesus did. I say this because I know the first few chapters of this book might seem a bit idealistic. On our own, with only "shoulds" to guide us, you'd be correct. But the Holy Spirit is a powerful force, lifting us above selfishness and small-mindedness and weak love to embrace the glorious strength of God loving through us. When the challenge of marriage casts us back upon God, we're in a good place. After the famous poet John Milton went blind, he wrote to a friend, "I do not even complain of my want of sight; in the night with which I am surrounded the light of the divine presence shines with a more brilliant luster."[1]

Milton believed God had to make him blind so that he could fully see the divine light; in the same way, God may allow us to come to the end of our own strength in marriage so that we might finally learn to rely on His.

Keep in mind: if your marriage and family feel like a joke or as if they're bordering on chaos, it's not anything that God hasn't seen or isn't capable of redeeming. So much of Christian teaching today is about us developing "our" gifts, improving "our" talents, reaching "our" potential, yet so much of Jesus's teaching and modeling is about surrendering to the work of the Holy Spirit. Let's allow marriage to teach us to trust this Holy Spirit. He's proven Himself. He won't go into retirement or even on vacation. He's not inexperienced or lacking in power or wisdom or understanding. We can trust Him. If we truly want to transform our marriages, we must learn the glory of divine dependence.

God will never call us to do something without giving us everything that is necessary in order for us to finish the task. It may not be all that we *think* we need, but it will be all that we *do* need. This is not to say the job will feel easy. But God promises through Isaiah, "He gives strength to the weary, and to him who lacks might He increases power" (Isa. 40:29 NASB). This verse assumes we are weary, so we must, on occasion, grow weary; it also assumes there is a task given to us for which we lack enough power on our own.

Don't pass over this thought, because it's crucial: *Isaiah 40:29 assumes that God will call us to various tasks for which we lack enough power on our own.*

The "secret," then, to a truly sacred marriage is actually a person, God's promised Holy Spirit. Because God is such a relational God (meeting our need for salvation by sending His Son), it shouldn't surprise us that He meets our need for transformation by also sending Himself in the person of His Holy Spirit: "You will receive power when the Holy Spirit comes on you" (Acts 1:8).

This isn't a Pentecostal truth or even a charismatic truth. It is a Christian truth: we all need the empowering work of the Holy Spirit. "What we have received is not the spirit of the world, but the Spirit who is from God, so that we may understand what God has freely given us. This is what we speak, not in words taught us by human wisdom but in words taught by the Spirit" (1 Cor. 2:12–13).

Since marriage is one of the most profound acts of worship any two believers can ever share, it is impossible to be married in a sacred manner without the Holy Spirit being active in our lives, helping us to understand what it means to love, giving us the power to love, convicting us when we fail to love, renewing our hearts when we grow weary in love, and pouring out hope when we grow discouraged in love. Rob Rienow wrote, "If you think you have it in you to be a godly husband, either you don't know what God desires, or you have set the bar way too low."[2]

The challenge of marriage is what sets us up for its glory: fostering a life of daily dependence on God. Any spouse who thinks he or she can live one day married as God calls us to be married without God sustaining, empowering, and equipping us is a man or woman who doesn't understand the high call of marriage. But here's the blessing hidden in the burden: new challenges and trials call out a new dependence, a new need for fresh power. When the challenges of marriage chase us into the arms of God, Satan loses and we win, big-time.

In his lectures to students, the great Baptist preacher Charles Spurgeon told the young men, "I am [wary] of anything which should hinder your daily dependence upon the Holy Spirit."[3] Yet how many marriage books fail to admit the impossibility of biblical marriage in our own strength? I want this book to point us to find another strength greater than our own—a marriage sustained by the Holy Spirit.

This isn't just theological speculation; there are enormous practical ramifications.

Who Are You Asking?

Many of you are frustrated in your marriages because you try to live as if the Trinity isn't part of the equation. You keep asking something of your spouse and rarely get it:

"Listen to me more."

"Talk to me more."

"Help out more."

"Have sex with me more often."

When was the last time you asked something of God's Holy Spirit? "Help me to love more. Help me to listen more. Renew my heart. Give me strength. Help me forgive …"

You'll have far more success and satisfaction in your marriage if you start asking more of God and less of your spouse.

Jesus teaches us to pray for the Holy Spirit to fill us, enlighten us, empower us, direct us, and renew us (Luke 11:13). According to Paul in Ephesians 5:18, we are to be continually "filled" with the Spirit. In the Greek this is an unusual construction called a present passive imperative: we are commanded to let something be done to us on an ongoing basis ("let yourself be continually filled with the Spirit").

I don't fill up my gas tank on Monday and then curse the automaker when I need to fill it back up on Friday. There isn't a car in existence that can keep going without refueling, and there isn't a marriage alive that can keep pressing into sacred intimacy without *daily* drawing on God's presence and power. This is one of the things I love about marriage, one area in which God shows His utter brilliance in designing it: our primary human relationship makes us dependent on our primary divine relationship every day.

Besides, God loves it when we ask for more of Him in the form of His Spirit. He promised to answer such prayers in dramatic fashion: "I will pour out my Spirit" (Acts 2:18). Notice He didn't say, "I will sprinkle my Spirit, drop by drop." God said He will *pour* out His Spirit.

It is the way of God with His people that He will often let us continue to fail and be frustrated until we learn to depend on Him. And that's the miracle of marriage—it forces us to depend on God, and all of life is transformed when we live in dependence on Him. It sets us up for success in literally every endeavor. No longer shackled to our natural gifts and resources (though these, too, come from our Creator), we are emboldened and empowered by a supernatural Presence.

We can keep trying to draw from an empty well, trying to transform our marriages by asking our stubborn or unfeeling spouses to meet our needs, or we can ask the God who promised to "pour out" His Spirit on all who seek Him for what they need.

Which do you think is the better use of our energy and effort? How many times have you said to your spouse, "We need to talk," thinking that talk will change your marriage? How few times have you knelt before your heavenly Father and said, "I need to listen"? Be wary of trying to talk it out with your spouse before you've prayed it out with your God.

Dependence, friends—dependence!

The Lawyer Who Became a Nurse

My friend Rett gulped deeply when the doctor told him and his wife, Kristy, that Kristy had to have a particular operation—one that could keep her in bed for several days and require special care for a few weeks after that.

Rett is a cognitive man, a brilliant lawyer, but he tends to live in his head with concepts and arguments and a quick wit. He makes a good living and can hire people to do what he doesn't want to do. He's not used to playing the role of a nurse, which is what he knew he would have to be doing for his wife.

On the way home from the doctor's office, Rett blurted out, "I don't know if I can do this!"

"What do you mean?" Kristy asked. "*I'm* the one getting the operation!"

"I mean, I don't know if I can be that low maintenance. I'm high maintenance. Tank (their dog) is high maintenance. The only reason our marriage works is because you're low maintenance and you hold everything together."

Marriage is a long journey—long enough so that eventually even the lower-maintenance spouse is going to be at least temporarily high maintenance. While many might see this a curse to bear, this really can be seen as a gift if the normally higher-maintenance spouse views such seasons as opportunities to step up and switch seats, becoming the primary caregiver.

In case you're wondering, Kristy gave Rett a glowing report about stepping up, though she admitted he was rather relieved when one of her relatives finally flew into town and took over.

Here's the key: marriage presented Rett with a situation he would never have chosen on his own. Rett didn't choose marriage to learn how to become a nurse—part of his attraction to Kristy was the fact that she was so low maintenance—but that's what he had to do now that he was a husband. Marriage called him to step up outside of himself, depend on Christ, and in the process become more like Christ.

Rett followed and appreciated Christ the teacher, but Jesus wasn't just a teacher. Christ touched the lepers, healed a woman who had been bleeding for years, and regularly made time out of His schedule to attend to the physical needs of those He loved. To put it in language Rett could now understand: Christ on earth wasn't just *cognitive*; He was also *caring*. For Rett to become like Christ, he had to grow in the same area. He had the cognitive down—you weren't going to trick him with false doctrine—but could he learn to care?

What is marriage calling you to right now, even today, that you don't feel capable of doing on your own? Instead of saying,

"This is just too hard" or "This just isn't my gifting or calling," why not hold God to His word? "Lord, You promise to give the weary strength. I am bone weary. You promise to give power to one who lacks it. I feel powerless. You promise to give the ignorant wisdom. I am clueless about what to do." Let's allow the difficulties of marriage to teach us the glory of spiritual dependence on God, tapping into that glorious, fierce force that exists outside ourselves.

A Fierce Force in Marriage

Many of us have experienced more than our fair share of good times in marriage, but even in the best of marriages, there will be moments when its inherent difficulty teaches us to depend on God with an entirely new force. Maturity comes from perseverance (see James 1:4), and perseverance assumes something is unpleasant. Because God designed marriage, at least in part, to work on our characters, we need to value the soul-scouring work of character building as much as we value the "easy" seasons of marriage.

Certainly, if God said to me, "Gary, I'm going to give you the easiest marriage and the easiest life anyone has ever known," I wouldn't be disappointed. While such a relationship might at times feel like a pleasant life, it might also cause me to miss out on an entirely different dimension: forcing me to tap into the power of Christ.

In 2 Corinthians 12:1–10, Paul presented a fundamental Christian truth: "My grace is sufficient for you, for my power is made perfect in weakness." Three times, Paul pleaded with God to remove his "thorn in the flesh." Three times God said, "My grace is sufficient for you, for my power is made perfect in weakness."

Paul got to the point where he said, "Therefore I will boast all the more gladly about my weaknesses, so that Christ's power may rest on me. That is why, for Christ's sake, I delight in weaknesses, in insults, in hardships, in persecutions, in difficulties. For when I am weak, then I am strong."

What if, instead of telling everyone how good we have it, we honestly testified to God's grace?

"We're really not compatible at all, but God has used those differences to build in us a humility we wouldn't have otherwise."

"We've never been comfortable financially, but that has kept us on our knees."

"We got married young, and the fact is, we both want different things out of life, but God is giving us grace and power every day to unite our hearts and keep us together."

"Blending two families has been brutal at times; neither of us believes we could have survived it without God giving us the strength day by day."

Is there a "thorn" in your marriage relationship that you have pleaded with God to take away many times? Is there something you wish He would heal but He hasn't?

"Really, God, we have to go through this issue again?"

In tough marital circumstances, do we seek resolution or do we seek Christ's power? Do we seek the pathway to an easier life or to a supernatural life? Will we accept that God may allow a thorn to remain in our lives to teach us the need for spiritual dependence?

It is in our weaknesses—as individuals and perhaps as couples—that Christ's power comes to rest on us; often it is only when we are at our end that we make way for God to begin. If God resolved every issue, every child's problem, and every spouse's annoyance with our first uttered prayer, we'd be weaker saints. We'd be weaker couples. We wouldn't display the power of Christ. Or we'd display it to a much lesser degree.

Can you thank God for that child who keeps you on your knees? Can you recognize why God may choose to allow the possibility of another addictive lapse to keep both of you living in dependence? Can you understand that God may not remove some difficulties that you hate because He wants you to rely on the supernatural power of Christ that He loves?

I believe it will change our marriages and our walks with God if we stop expecting every problem to be fixed and instead expect every difficulty to help us learn Paul's secret of strength in weakness.

"My grace is sufficient for you, for my power is made perfect in weakness."

Building a Lifelong Love

1. What is the greatest challenge in your marriage right now? Looking back, would you say this challenge is helping you to rely on God or is it tempting you to resent God?
2. How can believers fulfill the present passive imperative of Ephesians 5:18, continually allowing ourselves to be ever filled with the Spirit? How can marriage remind us of this command?

3. How might relying on the Holy Spirit change the way we approach a disagreement? Confront our spouses? Deal with ongoing family crises? Talk about what this biblical teaching looks like practically and how it might be "fleshed out"?

4. Have you, like Rett, come across a challenge in marriage that calls you to do something you don't feel you're particularly good at? How will you rely on the Holy Spirit to remain engaged in this challenge?

5. What challenges might God not be taking away from your life because you could become permanently stronger through them? Would you be okay if they never ended?

Gracious Giver of the Holy Spirit, thank You for creating a relationship so glorious and yet so difficult that we can't possibly live it on our own. Grant us the grace to become ever more dependent on You instead of ever more resentful when things aren't immediately "fixed" to our liking. If there is something within us—an act or an attitude, a faulty belief or a heart of rebellion—that is blocking us from being continually filled with Your Spirit, then please tear it down. Let us glory in our weaknesses that testify to Your provision instead of seeking comfort or ease that testify only to our selfishness. In Jesus's name, amen.

5

Got Mission?

When Kevin Miller asked his future wife, Karen, to marry him, her response was close to automatic. Later, Karen would admit that perhaps she should have thought a little more deeply about such a monumental life decision: "When Kevin popped the question—'Will you marry me?'—no one asked us a bigger question: 'Why do you want to get married?' At the time, the question would have bordered on blasphemy. After all, Kevin and I were in love—anyone could see that. We shared a commitment to Christ. Who needed better reasons than those?"[1]

The Millers, authors of *More Than You and Me*, then experienced what many Christian couples experience just a few years into marriage—a certain restlessness seeping into the relationship. It's nothing stunning, nothing earthshaking. It's just a quiet question: "Isn't there more to life than this? I mean, we love each other and all, but now that we've found each other, is this really all there is?"

This is life lived without a magnificent obsession. Some couples face the listlessness of self-absorption by thinking that they married the wrong person. If they had married someone else, perhaps the marriage would be more fulfilling. But the Millers found it wasn't about anything lacking in either one of them as people; it was about what they lacked as a couple in the sense of purpose. A lack of purpose is like a diseased heart that continually slows us down; a shared sense of purpose is like a defibrillation machine giving us another chance.

When a pastor asked them to take over the church youth group—a collection of out-of-control adolescents—Karen said, "The group literally drove us to our knees. Before each event, we began to pray for the youth and for ourselves. The group also forced Kevin and me to talk more than we had since we dated. We needed to plan together and present a united front to the kids. As we did, we found out a lot about each other."[2]

Here's one of the things I love about joint ministry: You think you know all about a person. You've been dating for a few years, married for another five, and it's easy to assume you've got everything figured out; there's nothing more to share, to discover, to talk about. Ministry of any significant kind raises a whole host of other issues; you see a side of yourself and each other that you never knew existed. Sometimes this can be inspiring, but other times it can be outright scary. The Millers attested that some of the challenges they faced and disagreements they suffered over how best to proceed at times felt like they would tear them apart as a couple. But the challenges made them talk, gave them a new reason to pray together, and a new intimacy was born. Purpose began to shock but save their marriage.

"The biggest surprise was that through the process something good was happening to our marriage. We were working together at something. When we failed, at least it was *our* failure; and when we succeeded, it was *our* success. During most of each workday, we were miles apart. But when we led the youth group, we were arm-in-arm and heart-to-heart."

Kevin and Karen gained a new respect for each other as they saw each other's gifts put to use, and they stumbled onto a great discovery: "What a puzzle! That youth group ministry, which by all rights should have pulled our marriage apart, actually bonded it in a new level of intimacy. Without trying to work on our marriage at all, it had become richer and deeper."[3]

The Third Hunger

It was in this context that the Millers discovered what they called a "third hunger." If you look at the book of Genesis, you can determine three aspects of marriage:

1. Companionship (Gen. 2:18: "It is not good for the man to be alone. I will make a helper suitable for him.")

2. Children (Gen. 1:28 NASB: "Be fruitful and multiply.")

Serving

3. Contribution (Gen. 1:28 NASB: "Fill the earth,
   and subdue it; and rule.")

In one sense, we could call this third aspect of Genesis "joint fulfilling service," the Old Testament equivalent of Matthew 6:33: "Seek first the kingdom of God" (ESV).

If our mission from Christ is to "seek first the kingdom of God," how can a successful, God-honoring marriage not be marked by mission? We're *not* told to seek first an intimate marriage, a happy life, obedient children, or anything else. Jesus tells us to seek first one thing, and one thing only: His kingdom and His righteousness (the two words define and build on each other, creating one common pursuit). A successful marriage is not only supported by a kingdom pursuit, but in many ways the pursuit is a prerequisite for postinfatuation intimacy.

The Millers understood, as I have come to understand, that life without this aim, and marriage without this purpose, is going to lose a lot of its luster. "We hunger for this today: cooperating together, meshing, working like a mountain climbing team, ascending the peak of our dream, and then holding each other at the end of the day. God has planted this hunger deep within every married couple. It's more than a hunger for companionship. It's more than a hunger to create new life. It's a third hunger, a hunger to do something significant together. According to God's Word, we were joined to make a difference. We were married for a mission."[4]

Being "married for a mission" can revitalize a lot of marriages in which the partners think they suffer from a lack of compatibility;

my suspicion is that many of these couples actually suffer from a lack of purpose. Jesus's words given to individuals in Matthew 6:33 are perhaps even truer in marriage. When we give away our life, we find it. When we focus outside our marriage, we end up strengthening our marriage.

A woman once wrote to *Marriage Partnership* magazine: "Over ten years of marriage, I have found that when my husband and I focus on our own needs, and whether they're being met, our marriage begins to self-destruct. But when we are ministering together, we experience, to the greatest extent we've known, that 'the two shall become one.'"[5]

Who Are You Married For?

Paul included an interesting little aside in his epistle to the Philippians. He warned them that so many "seek their own interests, not those of Jesus Christ" (2:21 ESV). If Paul were to examine your marriage, would he describe it as one that seeks your own interests or those of Jesus Christ?

When you try to serve your own interests in marriage rather than the interests of Jesus, you are likely to find that your marriage is making you less holy and, I would argue, eventually less happy too.

What are you honestly seeking first in your life? Whose interests are you preoccupied with? I love, love, love the conclusion the Millers came to in the early nineties as they surveyed a pile of Christian marriage books at a bookstore: "It's like we're telling

Christians to be single for the Lord but married for ourselves."[6] A sacred marriage calls us to be married for the Lord.

The First Prayer

Though every Christian marriage should ultimately aspire to seek God's kingdom as the primary mission, each couple will have a different expression of that mission. If you're raising kids, that, indeed, may be your first and longest mission. But a mission-minded marriage doesn't raise kids just for the sake of raising kids. Nor does a mission-minded marriage raise kids just to release two or three or four more selfish, consumer-minded narcissists into the world. A mission-minded marriage is focused on raising children who live in awe of God and who take their marching orders from Matthew 6:33, living their own magnificent obsession.*

Many couples practice and promote adoption. They have a difficult time talking about anything else and think every family should adopt. Our friend Annie, who has adopted five kids, once overheard Lisa and me just mention the *a* word (adoption) casually in a conversation with another couple. Annie practically ran across the room to say, "Oh, great! You *have* to do it. When

---

* We can't guarantee that every one of our children will adopt such a mission; one of Jesus's own disciples turned against Him in the end. But we can be faithful in our purpose and focus, and the struggle we face in the midst of that will unite us as surely as will "success."

can we meet? I can bring papers with me!" (That's a bit of an exaggeration, but not much.)

Others build businesses that employ families and serve in creative ways—they use their businesses as tools to serve the kingdom. Some couples are particularly active in the local church, or the arts community, or they reach out to sports-minded enthusiasts. The common link that you see in these couples is that their mission is what keeps their marriage vibrant on many levels. It's always all about the kingdom.

In so many ways, Jesus makes life simple and clear. If we seek to follow Jesus in our marriages, He even tells us how we should pray. Surely you remember that when the disciples asked Jesus to teach them to pray, Jesus responded, "When you pray, say: 'Father, hallowed be your name. *Your kingdom come*'" (Luke 11:2 ESV).

How many marital problems would be solved (or examined much differently) if our first prayer was always "Father, glorify Your name and bring Your kingdom rule to my heart, our marriage, and this house"?

Seriously, if we made that our first concern, our primary prayer, the starting point for resolution, wouldn't we look at everything differently?

Notice Jesus said this should be our first prayer, but how many couples have never really prayed this prayer second, tenth, or last? How often do we jump over this primary concern—the glory of God and the spread of His kingdom—to our pathetically trivial concerns? Our first prayer is far more likely to be

God's rule in my heart, then they kingdom come

"Lord, make him more pleasant!" "Lord, make her appreciate me!" "Lord, make him change!" "Oh yeah, and then, You know, after that, let Your kingdom come."

If our first concern really were the spread of God's rule in our hearts, and each prayer began with that entreaty, I suspect that we would handle most marital conflict 180 degrees differently from how we usually handle it. The resolution that we seek would be an entirely different aim. The tenor of our conversation would be refocused in some miraculous ways.

What if we tried this? What if the next time you and your spouse are at a heated point of disagreement, you join hands and pray, beginning with the words "Father, glorify Your name in this situation. Bring Your kingdom rule into our hearts. Help us look at this through the lens of what brings the most glory to You and what is evidence of our yielding our hearts to Your reign." And what if, in the listening and talking that followed, you and your spouse kept this prayer as your goal: How do we, in this situation, yield to God's reign? What attitude, decision, and action will bring Him the most glory?

Even better, what if we prayed this way outside of resolving conflict? What if we prayed to go on the offensive? "Lord, are we missing Your will, Your purpose? Have our eyes been blinded to something You really want to do through the two of us, working side by side in the day and holding each other at night?"

If you and your spouse are now empty nesters and have sensed a growing divide, why not ask yourselves, "Can we regather around a mission?* Can our hearts be knit back together by loving others whom God is calling us to love? And might not that joint service renew our own love?"

Some of you are no doubt screaming, "But that's the problem! We're already too busy, and now you want us to do *more*?" Perhaps you are too busy, but are you busy with the right things? Are you busy with a trivial obsession or a magnificent one? How can God bless an aimless house? Where is He supposed to "push" it—toward more comfort, more ease, more self-centered and apathetic happiness?

Purposeful Passion

How can you and your spouse discover *your* mission? Here's one exercise: Think forward to the end of your days and ask yourself, if you knew you were about to see God face-to-face, what would you most want to lay at His feet? What do you think He uniquely created you to do? And then ask, are you doing anything about that now?

---

* Some of you might well ask, "What if only one member of the couple cares about mission or we care about radically different missions?" To the first part of that question, we do what we can with a sweet, uncondemning spirit, not passively punishing our spouses for refusing to join us, but inviting them in by our firm and joyous resolve. To answer the second part of the question, there is no biblical law that the two of you must share the same mission and vision; there *is* biblical teaching that you should encourage and support each other, so focus on that.

It might be a joint effort, as it is with a couple we know who have been working for years to get a film made. It might be a vision in which you play a supporting role—such as a husband I know who has been his wife's business administrator, book table coordinator, and support extraordinaire as God has used his spouse to bless so many people. But it's something you are committed to *as a couple*.

Almost five hundred years ago, William Tyndale was burned at the stake solely for translating Scripture into an accessible language. One of his fiercest enemies wasn't some pagan chieftain but rather the king of England. During the tumultuous days of opposition that ultimately led to his imprisonment and death, Tyndale boldly told a clergyman, "If God spare my life, I will cause the boy that drives the plough to know more of the Scripture than you do."

You would think a clergyman would rejoice at such a declaration, but back then, you'd be wrong. It was considered scandalous and even a capital offense. Though Tyndale's life was cut short, the seed that Tyndale had nurtured took hold and his mission was accomplished; easily accessible versions of Scripture soon covered the European continent and laid the groundwork for the English Reformation.

It all began with a mission. Tyndale could see it, taste it, and picture it. By getting the Scriptures into an accessible language, a common boy could know the Scriptures as well as any clergyman. It was a mission Tyndale literally laid down his life to achieve.

Exercise

Here's a good date-night idea: Discuss how you and your spouse would finish Tyndale's statement, "If God spare my life …" What's your dot-dot-dot? What would you most like to see happen?

That's a good indicator of what your mission might be. A common mission is a powerful tool of marital intimacy. Many of you will discover that the more you are engaged in purposeful spiritual conflict, the less you will be sidetracked by petty marital conflict. There is a reason Jesus said, "Seek first his kingdom and his righteousness, *and all these things will be given to you* …" (Matt. 6:33). Try it, and you'll see.

Building a Lifelong Love

1. Have you ever asked yourself the question Karen Miller asked herself: "Why did we get married?" Why *do* you think you got married? *Believed God brought us together for a purpose... to serve and glorify others...*

2. What has been your primary marital mission up till now? Do you have one? *Align each member of our family w/ God's purpose — to glorify Him in our days and our endeavors*

3. Paul wrote to the Philippians that some seek their own interests instead of those of Jesus Christ. In your marriage, whose interests are you seeking most? *This has become convoluted for me. Too often we have missed the mark by hyperfocusing on the trivial...*

4. Does your first prayer most commonly line up with Jesus's first prayer? Will you begin opening up your prayers in line with how Jesus taught us to pray? *No. "Seek ye first the Kingdom of God." Yes. Lord, please rule in my heart so that it is Your will to be done, Your Kingdom come. He is honored.*

5. Set aside a date night to discuss possible "marital missions"—long-term and short-term. Pray about how you and your spouse would finish the thought "If God spare our lives, then …" *what?*

Heavenly Father, regardless of why we got married, we pray that ~~we~~ our *will begin adopting Your agenda for the rest of our lives together. Teach us to pray as Your Son taught us to pray—seeking first Your kingdom. Help us to understand the unique purpose You have for us, as individuals and as a couple, and help us to be faithful in accomplishing that purpose. We pray that we would start living with Your interests in mind, even above our own. Renew our relationship with the excitement of rejoining around a common spiritual purpose. This is what You made us for, and we pray that You would grant us the grace to surrender to that call. In Jesus's name, amen.*

6

A Monk's Marriage

While vacationing in France, my wife and I got a personal tour of a twelfth-century castle, passed down through family after family. The duke, well into his eighties, took a liking to my wife and insisted on walking us around, much to our delight. He and his wife openly argued about the need to restore the moat. The duke's view was that a proper castle must have a proper moat. His wife shook her head and simply said, "Mosquitoes."

Inside the family chapel, the duke pulled my wife aside and said, "Would you like to see my ancestors?"

Dumbfounded as to what he could mean, Lisa said, "Sure."

He opened up the lid of a bench Lisa was standing next to and showed her three collections of bones, complete with skulls.

An ancestor of the duke had avoided assassination during the French Revolution, but you could see the scars of rebellion on the castle walls. The duke explained the crowd's anger: in the days prior to the revolution, dukes had unfettered power over their duchies. They could sentence anyone to death, and there was no appeal process. It was tyranny unchained, and when the taste of freedom from one man's arbitrary rule took hold, there was no holding the people back.

In a similar way, when the book of Psalms was written, kings determined who lived and who died, which towns were built and which were destroyed, who feasted and who starved. These rulers could claim your fields, your wife or husband, your daughters and sons. Speaking of Nebuchadnezzar, Daniel said, "All the peoples, nations and men of every language feared and trembled before him; whomever he wished he killed and whomever he wished he spared alive; and whomever he wished he elevated and whomever he wished he humbled" (Dan. 5:19 NASB). All of this makes Psalm 146 (which actually has a lot to say about marriage by implication) an unusually radical call.

The psalmist said straight-out, "Do not trust in princes, in mortal man, in whom there is no salvation" (v. 3 NASB). This doesn't sound shocking to us, but most people when this was written would have gone to great lengths to find favor with the prince; in many ways the prince *could* offer salvation—or at least seem to. It was like reading today, "If you get into trouble with the law, don't worry about the police, the judge, or the lawmaker—just pray."

The psalmist reminded the people that the king was simply a man who would die (v. 4), and when he died, everything he had, including their favor with him, would die too—and then where would they be? In contrast, the psalmist said, "Blessed is he whose help is the God of Jacob, whose hope is in the LORD" (v. 5 NASB).

Why? Well, let's see. God made all that is (v. 6); He provides justice for the oppressed, food for the hungry, freedom for prisoners, healing for the sick, and encouragement for the discouraged (vv. 7–8); He "thwarts the way of the wicked," and His reign, far from ending at death, will be "forever … to all generations" (vv. 9–10 NASB).

We can't understand this psalm unless we realize that it made perfect sense to the people in that day to trust in the earthly king whom they could see rather than some deity whom they could not. This was a radical realignment of trust and dependency.

Today, many of us choose to trust in spouses we can see rather than a God we cannot. If we're lonely, why aren't our spouses more relational? If we're poor, why don't our spouses work harder or contribute more? If we're sick, why aren't our spouses better caretakers? If we're discouraged, why aren't our spouses more empathetic? It makes perfect sense to us to look to our spouses first, but to trust in mortal man (or woman) rather than the immortal God is to spurn the One who rules heaven and earth in favor of one whose body will, sooner rather than later, become part of the earth.

We are to love our spouses, and that is very different from depending on our spouses. We are to put our trust in the God we can't see—even if that feels counterintuitive—because it's far wiser to do that than to trust in one we can see whose power (and character) is so severely limited.

If you're tempted to say, "But my spouse *should* do x or y," consider this: What if your spouse had a severe stroke from which he or she never fully recovered? Would you expect anything of your spouse then? Wouldn't you then be forced to rely on God? That's what this psalmist was saying. To trust in mortal man or woman, to depend on them, is to trust in one whose days are limited and whose influence will perish. Eventually, you will have to do without your spouse, one way or another. So learn to trust in God now. Though this may sound bizarre until I explain it, we need to be married people with a monk's heart.

Married Like a Monk

Fourteenth-century Augustinian Canon Regular Walter Hilton mimicked many classical writers when he urged believers to pursue the spirit of detachment, to the point where we literally "put no kind of trust in the possession of any worldly goods, or in the help or favor of any worldly friend, but principally and entirely in God. For if he does otherwise, he binds himself to the world, and therefore he cannot be free to think about God."*

This might seem a tad difficult in marriage, and theologically, you might even (quite correctly, in one sense) consider it an attack on Christian community and fellowship. However, it does contain some helpful and profound advice for marriage.

Isn't it true that many marital arguments result from disappointment with our spouses? We want them to be something or

---

* I wrote a whole chapter on the discipline of spiritual detachment in an old book of mine titled *The Glorious Pursuit: Embracing the Virtues of Christ* (Colorado Springs: NavPress, 1998).

do something or catch something and they aren't or they don't, and we feel sorry for ourselves. We really do want them to love us like God loves us. We expect them to just know when we've had a hard day; to know that we're lying when we say, "Don't worry. It's no big deal. I don't need anything special"; to know that we need them to be strong or soft, to yield or to hold firm, just because that's what we need them to do. If they truly loved us, they would know, right?

Be honest: Don't you think or feel that way sometimes?

And you do recognize that's an impossible burden for a human spouse, right?

But what if I sought a "monk's marriage"? What if I decided that I would depend on God alone, expecting nothing from my spouse but depending entirely on God for all my needs, including emotional and relational needs?

Then, instead of resenting what my spouse doesn't do, I'll be overwhelmed (in a good way) by every little thing she does do. I'll be filled with gratitude instead of resentment. In 2010, after fifteen years of self-employment, I was hired as writer-in-residence at Second Baptist Church in Houston, Texas. On my first day, I was blown away when a church staff member said, "We need to give you a new phone and a new laptop." As a self-employed person, nobody had purchased anything for me for more than a decade; why was Second Baptist going to give these things to me when they were already providing a paycheck? I found out there were security reasons: they needed the laptop and phone set up in such a way to make sure sensitive church information wasn't compromised, and they also wanted to make sure that my platforms were compatible with those of the rest of the church staff. Still, I kept thinking, *They're not only paying me; they're giving me free stuff!*

I can imagine, though, as time wears on, that I might start thinking, *When do I get a new laptop? This one is getting kind of old. And my old phone battery now has to be charged three times a day!*

In that moment, I'll move from gratitude to resentment, because I'll have begun expecting what used to delight me.

Isn't that exactly what happens in marriage? When you're dating someone and he does something nice for you, you think, *How wonderful!* If you marry him and he doesn't reach a certain threshold of gift giving, you think, *This is all he got me? Seriously?*

That's why I want a "monk's marriage," the benefits of being married to a godly woman, but with a monk's attitude, expecting nothing, depending on God, and so being genuinely grateful for whatever my spouse chooses to bless me with.

I realize we can take this too far. God won't fertilize your yard when your husband is watching the game. God won't meet our sexual needs. There are duties that seem reasonable that we want our spouses to meet, but put this in another context: Do you expect a spouse who has a broken back to fertilize your yard? Do you expect a woman in a severe state of Alzheimer's to meet your sexual needs? The time may come when your spouse simply can't meet those "legitimate" needs, and what will you do then?

Now let's ask, if it's "can't meet those needs" or "won't meet those needs," does it really matter, as far as our call to love them is concerned? Aren't we allowing them to hold our contentment hostage in either case?

This might, indeed, be a little too "spiritual," but I think there's a lot of freedom to be found in pursuing a monk's marriage somewhere along the line. Let's look at how this played out with ancient writers from the East. There's still a bit more to explore here.

Pride and the Love of Praise

If you're from the West and alive to read this, the *Philokalia* was written in another time and a world away. Its audience was the Eastern world, and its main writers were celibate desert monks, hermits, ascetics, and champions of Eastern Orthodox spirituality who explored the deeper life. I realize I test the patience of some readers by so regularly quoting from nonevangelical sources, but in this instance, please consider the substance (instead of the source), as the *Philokalia* has challenged me to view my pride—particularly within marriage—through an entirely fresh perspective.

The *Philokalia* persistently—almost obsessively—warns against the love of praise and esteem by others, calling this lust one of the gravest spiritual ills, one of three poisonous passions through which all other sins flow. There's a lot of Bible for these writers to follow: "[We did not] seek praise from mortals, whether from you or from others" (1 Thess. 2:6 NRSV). "For am I now seeking the approval of man, or of God? Or am I trying to please man? If I were still trying to please man, I would not be a servant of Christ" (Gal. 1:10 ESV). There are plenty more verses we could choose from.

Even so, many of the pastoral calls I receive from married people concern a spouse who isn't getting what he or she wants from the other spouse. The monks may be on to something here—their warnings may be even truer in marriage. Isn't the lust for praise the spiritual disposition that ruins so much marital satisfaction?

"Notice me!"

"Appreciate me!"

"Thank me!"

"Don't take me for granted!"

"He doesn't even see me anymore!"

"I can't remember the last time she was affectionate toward me!"

We think of these sentiments as "rights" rather than as temptations, so we read marriage books and go to marriage seminars hoping that, at last, our spouses will "get it." In the *Philokalia*, these spiritual demands are evidence of hearts subject to idolatry, not yet set on and content in God. They are proof that we are looking to the world for something that we find only in the divine relationship.

If I believe in the judgment seat of Christ, I will live to please Him on that most glorious of days. As we stated earlier, it won't be about whether I was noticed, but whether I noticed. It won't be about whether I was encouraged, but whether I encouraged.

If we accept that the love of praise is a sin, that the lust to be noticed and appreciated by others is not just a fool's errand (can we ever be appreciated enough?) but perhaps evidence of a heart focused on the wrong things, our marriages will be transformed.

We'll become God focused, turning our hearts to the spiritual commandment to love instead of giving in to the lust to be loved.

What I'm about to say is going to sound so revolutionary to some of you that it may start a fight, but I hope instead it will begin a healthy discussion. From the perspective of the *Philokalia*, lust isn't just when a husband mentally undresses another woman; lust is when the husband chews on resentment because it's been so long since his wife has thanked him for working so hard. Lust isn't just when a wife sighs when Ryan Gosling removes his shirt; lust is when the wife demands that her husband consider her more beautiful than all other women. It is the lust of wanting, even demanding, to be praised, thanked, noticed.

Do I live to please humans, to be noticed by them and appreciated by them, or do I live to please God? Reread Galatians 1:10 and see how important this is. We think the problem is our spouses' insensitivity, apathy, even cruelty. Time and again, both Scripture and the Christian classics point us back to our pride as the real enemy of marriage and Christlikeness.

Think about this, even try it out: What is more likely to lead to true marital satisfaction—getting a fallen spouse to change his or her ways, or changing your own focus so that you draw your affirmation from a God who never disappoints, never turns you away?

The Red Room

Back in France, the duke and duchess took us to the "red room." Every proper castle had to have a room decorated in red, set aside for the king. If the king were traveling through the country, he'd go to the nearest castle and know there would be a red room set aside only for him.

I love the image of a room in our house set aside for the arrival of the King. All that we've been talking about is geared toward allowing God as our King to rule in our actions, our minds, and our affections—especially our affections. What if we spent more time readying a room in our hearts to receive our King rather than chasing our spouses' affections and finding them wanting? These aren't opposing pursuits, of course—we can do both; but what if we focused a little more on the former instead of putting all our hope in the latter?

Perhaps you'll find what I have found—the less I expect from my spouse in this regard, the more I appreciate her. This practice has *increased* my affections immeasurably, making me newly sensitive to every received kindness instead of bitterly resentful over every perceived withholding.

✱ Build a red room, and invite the King's presence into the home of your heart.

Building a Lifelong Love

1. What does Psalm 146 teach us about the dangers of allowing a fallen human being—even a spouse—to have so much power over our affections, our sense of acceptance, and our life satisfaction?

2. How do we distinguish between healthy desire and mutual dependence within marriage, and the lust to be noticed and appreciated?

Expectations were less w/ [handwritten]

3. Why were we so grateful for the little things our spouses did *[handwritten]* when they were still boyfriends and girlfriends, when we are *[handwritten]* now so ungrateful for the things they do as our spouses? How *[handwritten]* do we avoid taking our spouses for granted? *[handwritten: lowering expectations and loving, listening, attending ...]*

4. Of course, it is still legitimate to discuss both needs and wants with a spouse, but how might the discipline of detachment affect the spirit and attitude of such discussions?

5. What can you begin doing to draw more affirmation from your God so that you're less demanding of your spouse?

God of our delight, make us newly sensitive to the treasures of Your love, acceptance, and affirmation. Overwhelm us with a sense of how sufficient Your love is to fill our souls and comfort our hearts. As impossible as it may sound to us not to trust in people for what we need, please lead us along the journey of Psalm 146 to gradually place more and more of our trust and dependence on You. May we know the joys and intimacies of marriage while also experiencing the spiritual delights of detachment. We pray this in Jesus's name, amen.

7

A Marriage Worthy of Our Calling

"Gary, I really need a new purse. Mind if we go check those out?"

I saw the clearance sign and said, "Sure. No problem."

I had never shopped for purses before. There was a colossal ignorance in my life about this somewhat secretive practice among women.

Let me put this in perspective.

As one who has traveled more than 1.3 million miles on one airline (unfortunately the one that is usually rated worst by *Forbes*), I buy several suitcases a year. I've learned that the more expensive brands don't hold up much better than the "normal" brands you can get at a sharply reduced rate at, say, T.J. Maxx or Marshalls. Typically, I'll walk out of the store with a twenty-eight-inch suitcase with a collapsible handle, wheels, lots of zippered pockets, and usually an inside pouch for around a hundred bucks.

So when I walked up to a table of clearance purses, all of which could hold only about one-tenth of what I could fit in my suitcase, had no hardware, no metal handles, no wheels, and far fewer zippers (or none), I was naturally thinking they might cost one-tenth the price.

I couldn't have been more wrong.

Six hundred bucks. Fifteen hundred bucks! Eight hundred bucks. *On clearance.*

Men, you need to know, when our wives talk to us about buying a new purse, they're really asking, "Can we take out a second mortgage?"

Lisa didn't pay those prices, though we did pay more than I would for a suitcase, even though we could have fit ten of her purses inside that one suitcase.

The purses are seen as valuable, however, in part because they cost so much. It's a marketing gimmick that has worked very well for this industry. Why a purse costs more than a suitcase mystifies me, but I've never been one to understand fashion.

Some women wouldn't be caught without a purse that is "worthy" of their station in life. I've got my own occasional indulgences (running gear), so I'm not going to get into that. Even more than we want a purse or piece of clothing that is worthy of our calling in life, I'd like us to talk about building a *marriage* that is worthy of our calling.

Consider this passage from Ephesians 4:1–3:

> Therefore I … beg you to lead a life worthy of your calling, for you have been called by God. Always be humble and gentle. Be patient with each other, making allowance for each other's

faults because of your love. Make every effort to keep yourselves united in the Spirit, binding yourselves together with peace. (NLT)

What if we focused just one phrase of this passage to make it read like this:

I beg you to *build a marriage* worthy of your calling. Always be humble and gentle. Be patient with each other, making allowance for each other's faults because of your love. Make every effort to keep yourselves united in the Spirit, binding yourselves together with peace.

The notion of building a marriage "worthy of our calling" recognizes that we have been enlisted in the most glorious work ever known: the advancement of God's kingdom, what we have been calling the "magnificent obsession." This gives not only a certain dignity to our marriages but also something to aim for. Happiness is a wonderful thing and an understandable goal, but a magnificent obsession is even bigger (not at war with our happiness, just bigger). Wanting to build a marriage "worthy of my calling" motivates me to work on creating a certain kind of marriage dedicated to a very particular purpose.

To have a marriage worthy of our calling, we need to be, according to Paul's words in Ephesians 4, humble and gentle. Pause for a moment here: How did Jesus describe Himself in Matthew

11:29? Keep in mind that Jesus almost never used virtues to describe Himself, preferring instead to use images (the light of the world, the gate, the good shepherd, and so forth). In the one instance where Jesus did use virtues, He said, "I am gentle and humble in heart."

So, *creating a marriage worthy of my calling means creating a marriage where the character of Jesus is displayed for all to see.* More than we should seek to build the kind of marriage *we* want, we should seek to build the kind of marriage that serves our calling, and that means building marriages in which we are gentle with our spouses, because Jesus is gentle with His church. We are to be humble, because Jesus was humble.

Without this instruction, we might never aspire to gentleness or humility. We may prefer compatibility or security or even something as wonderful as laughter. There is nothing wrong with these things, but there is something seriously wrong with the lack of gentleness and humility. Yet not once have I ever gotten an email or an office visit from a couple asking me, "How can we be more gentle and humble in our relationship?"

So marriages that aspire to be worthy of our calling are marriages where we do not act or speak harshly with each other. We do not "lord it" over one another, swallowing each other up with our own expectations or dreams. We are servants, mutually caring for each other. That's what best models our calling. When people see the way we treat each other, they are reminded of Jesus.

When Paul wrote these words to a Greek audience, he knew that the culture despised humility, yet he extolled it for this reason: Jesus showcased humility, so we must showcase humility as we seek to proclaim Jesus to the world. Pride kills relationship and devastates a marriage. Pride is unworthy of our calling to proclaim a Savior who "made himself nothing by taking the very nature of a servant" (Phil. 2:7).

Do you see the difference? Instead of trying to build a marriage I want, a magnificent obsession leads me to seek to build the kind of marriage that reveals Jesus to the world.

Paul tells us we are also to be "patient with each other, making allowance for each other's faults because of your love." We've read James 3:2 ("We all stumble in many ways"), so we know our partners will falter at times. But because of the love within us by God's Holy Spirit, we make allowances for each other rather than judging each other. *We show the world that Christian couples treat sin with grace.* "Making allowance" means we are sensitive and encouraging about each other's weaknesses and idiosyncrasies, the quirkiness of our natures that sometimes needs to be accommodated. We do this with joy and a good spirit. God created our spouses, so it is a joy to worship Him by celebrating this unique expression of His creative genius.

This calls us to a nurturing marriage instead of an attacking marriage. So many couples get obsessed with how their spouses are failing and how much they have to put up with. We should have the concern of a physician, wanting them to get well, rather than the passion of a prosecuting attorney, wanting to make them pay. Yes, they may throw up on us, bleed on us, or even cry out in pain when we offer a healing injection. All the time, we ought to make allowances for them rather than judge them—not because that makes life easier for us, but because that's the kind of marriage that is worthy of our calling.

John Stott called these attitudes in Ephesians 4:1–3 the "five foundation stones" of Christian unity: humility, gentleness, patience, forbearance, and love. This is what marks our marriages as "worthy of our calling." Sometimes we may have to apply this unilaterally (without our spouses' cooperation).

Also note—this is so key—that, because of our calling, Paul urges us to make every effort—think about that—*every* effort to keep ourselves united in the Spirit. We are called to a ministry of reconciliation—God reconciling the world to Himself, us demonstrating that by being reconciled to each other—so we give everything we've got as we depend on the Spirit's empowerment to keep ourselves united in the Spirit. We talk things through. We forgive. We don't stonewall. We pursue reconciliation and under-standing. Again, not because this is the easy life, but because it is the only life worthy of our calling.

So what does this mean? I am dedicated to the preservation of my marriage's unity. Not just for my happiness and my chil-dren's security, but because of my calling in Christ. I will guard my marriage, feed it, work through issues, confront when necessary if something is threatening our unity, forgive with eagerness to preserve our unity, be gentle so that no bitterness attacks our unity, live with patience so that I don't replay past episodes, and certainly remain vigilant to never let my heart be stolen by anyone else.

So many people seek to build a "happy" marriage. That's fine. God is into happiness. But even more, I want to build a marriage that is "worthy of my calling." Why not build a marriage that seeks to remind people of Jesus?

Building a Lifelong Love

1. What has motivated you to want to make changes in your marriage: your own happiness, or a desire to build a marriage worthy of your calling?
2. Why do we tend not to value gentleness and humility and perseverance as much as Scripture calls us to? What do most couples focus on above these traits?
3. To build a marriage that more accurately reveals Jesus to the world, the husband and wife need humility, gentleness, patience, forbearance, and love. What do you and your spouse most need to work on? If you had to choose just one thing, what would it be?
4. Would you say you have an attacking marriage or a nurturing marriage?

Our most worthy God, we are blessed indeed to be able to call ourselves Your children and to be invited to participate in Your work on this earth. Give us hearts that desire to build a marriage worthy of this high calling. Make us long for a marriage that more accurately reveals Jesus to those who don't know Him. Help us see where we fall short—open our blind eyes, give us a new thirst for the things that You value (humility, gentleness, patience, love) and less hunger for the lesser things that so many people focus on. In Jesus's name, amen.

8

Do Your Duty: The Surprising Call to Happiness

Let's review everything we've learned in this section:

- Placing our marriages within the framework of a magnificent obsession
- Recognizing God as our heavenly Father-in-Law
- Worshipping our way to happiness
- Learning to live in a state of spiritual dependence on God
- Pursuing spiritual mission to preserve marital passion
- Remembering how judgment day should impact this day

- Practicing the spiritual discipline of detachment to serve satisfaction
- Building a marriage worthy of our calling

All of this can now come together to a central point: if we want a *lifelong love*, a marriage that grows in love rather than disappointment, a marriage that gets ever closer rather than ever more estranged, a marriage that is moving forward rather than stuck in place, we need to root our actions within marriage in something so rock solid that we can't lose sight of these precious eternal truths. Paul gives us this something in Ephesians 5:21 when he tells us we are to relate to each other "out of reverence for Christ."

This brings us right back to worship, the heart of our magnificent obsession.

There was no stronger call in Paul's mind than to treat someone out of reverence for Christ. Christ always deserves to be reverenced; there will never be a millisecond in this universe when Jesus isn't King of Kings, conquering hero, and triumphant Savior. Which means, if our motivation to love is always based on reverence for a God who always deserves to be reverenced, our motivation can't possibly fail. Nothing can ever shake it.

So later, when Paul said men should love their wives as Christ loved the church (Eph. 5:25), he was saying this was an obligation, not a favor. Love doesn't have to be earned. Our wives don't have to "deserve" it. A Christian husband doesn't love his wife only when she is lovable. He loves her whenever Christ deserves to be reverenced, which, of course, is always.*

Women, Paul is just as bold with you: "The wife must respect her husband" (v. 33). Did you catch that little word "must"? Not even *should*, but *must*. Your response to your husband is to be based on Christ and the church (vv. 22–33), not your husband's character.

Which is why early church father John Chrysostom cut through all our objections when he wrote, "Do your duty! A wife should respect her husband even when he shows her no love, and a husband should love his wife even when she shows him no respect."[1]

We can't do our spouses' duties, so it is wasted time to fret over whether they are doing their part. Chrysostom urges us to focus instead on doing *our* part. This is what reverence to Christ calls us to—it removes our commitment to and practice of marriage from the changing whims of a sinful world (including a sinful partner) and places it on the never-changing foundation of reverence for Christ.

I find it most helpful to resolve to myself once and for all that this is just the way it is. No argument. No rationalizing. No searching for a onetime exclusion. If I call myself a Christian, I have certain marital obligations that not even my wife can discharge me from. I am to love my wife not as she deserves, necessarily, but as Christ loves the church (Eph. 5:25). Women, you are to submit to

---

* Of course, God's love can result in seemingly harsh consequences. Don't confuse the word *love* here with *nice*. Sometimes husbands have to step up and challenge their recalcitrant wives, as wives must sometimes step up and challenge their recalcitrant husbands.

your husbands not on the basis of their being pleasant and kind, but "as the church submits to Christ" (v. 24). (How you define and apply the word "submit" is a discussion for another time.)

We do our duty, therefore, because marriage isn't primarily about us but about Christ and the church. Marriage is a picture of the gospel before it is a vehicle of happiness. It's a prophetic call and duty before it is a playground of romanticism. It's a serious business, not a sentimental act of whimsy.

We will never understand Paul's words to husbands and wives unless we understand his primary motivation—that it's not about happiness or fulfillment but the proclamation of the gospel. This is so clear in Titus: "[The older women] can urge the younger women to love their husbands and children, to be self-controlled and pure, to be busy at home, to be kind, and to be subject to their husbands, *so that no one will malign the word of God*" (2:4–5). We are so obsessed with what Paul meant (and didn't mean) by that one word, "subject," that we miss the whole point: "so that no one will malign the word of God." We entirely miss the magnificent obsession behind Paul's passionate teaching. If we don't understand Paul's motivations, we'll never understand his instructions. It's like telling a wide receiver how to run his routes without ever explaining that, in the end, it's all about catching the ball.

"But, Coach, why do I have to cut? What do you mean by cut? Why are you so obsessed with whether I cut? What if I'd be happier running a slow fade?" No doubt the coach wants to scream, "*Just get open and catch the ball!*"

In Paul's mind, marriage isn't about rights as much as it is about revelation.

This sense of doing our duty doesn't squeeze the romance or enjoyment out of marriage; on the contrary, it preserves it. It lifts us above our petty sinful natures and places the success of our marriages on the perfection of Jesus rather than on our spouses' performance and imperfection. Marriages based on superficial commitments like a person's behavior are doomed to rise or fall with a spouse's mood and momentary decisions. Marriages based on the eternal relationship of Christ and the church will share the same delight and joy that the latter have for each other (which, by the way, is deliciously intense). In this sense, ironically enough, the call to "do your duty" isn't just a call to holiness; it's a call to true happiness.

Not Just a Kiss

Recently, my wife joined me to tour the facilities of a Christian ministry that had invited me to speak at an upcoming benefit dinner. We saw all they were doing and the lives they were touching, and we talked about the goals for the dinner. I prayed for the executive staff and the upcoming dinner, and then Lisa and I got into separate cars to go to two different places.

I had heard the executive director praising Lisa for taking care of so many details in preparation for the banquet. I saw Lisa's respect as she looked at me in a ministry situation. We weren't just husband and wife—we were brother and sister in Christ, partners in the work God has called us to.

Our cars were parked side by side. Lisa rolled her passenger side window down, so I did the same. She said some nice things and then blew me a kiss, which I returned.

This was after twenty-nine years of marriage. We were knocking on the door of three decades of being together. Our affection was renewed by a common call greater than our happiness, greater than our comfort, financial situation, or anything else. Together, we were serving the King of Kings, and our marriage has benefited enormously. We are most happy when we are most focused on serving God together.

That's not why we serve the King, but that's the result of serving the King together. The spiritual component of marriage isn't a paint job on a car; it's the engine that makes the car move. Spending so much time on the spiritual aspect of marriage might seem somewhat divorced from reality, but I believe it is the most practical truth we can lay hold of. Once you make honoring God in your marriage a priority, all the practical day-to-day decisions become easy. "My husband left his towel on the floor again; should I 'forget' to make his coffee tomorrow morning?" When you commit to honoring God, these questions are not even questions anymore—you should always serve your spouse.

Living life in a way that is worthy of the call of Christian marriage is our top priority. Doing "our duty" is the only thing that will lead to true marital happiness and satisfaction—regardless of what our circumstances or spouses' response may be.

That's not to suggest there isn't more to say. Remember, the magnificent obsession is just one leg of a three-legged stool.

The next leg is learning how, as a couple, we can keep growing together in ever-increasing intimacy. That's what we've saved for part 2.

Building a Lifelong Love

1. Of the points listed at the beginning of this chapter, which ones have been most helpful for you? Which ones would you most like to grow in?
2. If our commitment to our marriages is based on our reverence for Christ, what does this say about the centrality of worship? How do you think you're doing in this area?
3. What did you think of this statement: marriage is not about anyone's rights as much as it is about revelation. Do you agree or disagree? How so?
4. Are you doing "your duty"? Do you believe that this could lead you to true marital satisfaction regardless of the way your spouse responds?

Lord Jesus, it is our highest honor and joy to live out of reverence for You. Give us new eyes and new minds to see how glorious You truly are. Give us hearts that live in awe of the honor and glory You represent. And then please give us wills that will love out of the force of that reverence. Give us attitudes that are cleansed by the purpose of that reverence. Give us lives that will seek to protect, proclaim, and preserve that reverence. It's in Your name that we pray, amen.

Part Two

Growing Together

A More Intimate Union

[handwritten note in margin: no couple is ever called to be the same!]

"No man is ever called to be another. God has as many plans for men as he has men; and, therefore, he never requires them to measure their life exactly by way of any other life."[1]

With these words, nineteenth-century churchman Horace Bushnell said something profound of individuals that is just as true of married couples, so let me put this in the language of marriage: "No married couple is ever called to be another. God has as many plans for married couples as He has couples; and, therefore, He never requires them to measure their life by any other couple."

You comprise one-half of a unique couple. No other couple has your gifts, your weaknesses, your history, your dynamics, your children, your calling. There is great freedom in accepting our couple identity as it is: we might be strong in this area, weak in that, vulnerable here, impenetrable there, excelling in this, often failing in that, but we are a unique couple called forth by God to fulfill our unique purpose in this world.

God has established your home and your marriage, *and that's the life He wants you to live.* Never look to other couples to measure your worth; look to God to fulfill your call. Don't compare yourself with other couples to measure your happiness; compare your obedience with God's design on your life to measure your faithfulness.

Lisa and I are not called to be Les and Leslie Parrott, who have two PhDs (Lisa and I have, between the two of us, none) and who write and speak jointly (Lisa often likes to say, "Nobody asks plumbers' wives if they can fix a toilet, so why does everyone ask me if I will give a talk just because my husband does?"). We are not called to be like Dr. Ed and Jo Beth Young, or Rick and Kay Warren, couples who lead two of the largest churches in the country, beloved by their congregations of more than thirty years for their rock-solid, stay-in-one-place leadership. We've moved around a good bit; our kids don't really have one place they can call "home."

We are not called to be like our friends Doug and Julie, who, with their financial resources, can literally choose which ministries to help launch in which countries that God has laid on their hearts.

We're just Gary and Lisa. That's all we're called to be. We have no other map to follow, no other marriage to live up to, no other couple that should make us feel ashamed, humiliated, envious, or proud. We don't have to live up to them, and they don't have to live up to us.

We will never have the financial resources that some other couples have; yet we also do not bear the financial anxieties that many poorer couples face. Neither one of us feels like we are particularly adept at handling money, so we're glad that God has given us enough but not too much.

We don't have a startling testimony or something major we've had to overcome. There haven't been (as of yet) any huge medical crises. We've just sought to live the life that God has given us, in large part because there's no other life to live.

Become comfortable with *your* story, *your* identity as a couple. Relish it. Never compare it. Just be faithful to the unique vision

God has given to the unique you (and that's a plural *you*). God doesn't need another couple just like one He has already made. He is so much more creative than that. Rather, He wants to release and bless the unique couple that is *you*.

This section is all about the two of you continuing to grow together as a couple as part of your own unique journey. It's not about me laying out a blueprint for what I think your marriage should be, but rather the two of you taking hold of what God created you to be to pursue a more intimate union. I believe this has to be intentional, thoughtful, and prayerful.

9

Supernatural Science

Science and the supernatural are usually touted as enemies or even exclusive realities. Talking about "supernatural science," then, seems like a contradiction in terms.

But sometimes, it's just true.

When Lauren Fleshman crushed a two-mile race in her junior year of high school, she earned an all-expenses-paid trip to the Olympic Training Center in San Diego. The OTC is designed to identify, train, and test promising young athletes for the Olympic Games, and Lauren seemed like the perfect candidate.

Until, that is, the scientific tests came back.

Her skin-fold test was a source of embarrassment (even though she looked skinny), and her hemoglobin and hematocrit counts revealed her to be borderline anemic. The one test, though, that really counts, the one that many researchers believe sets a hard limit on a middle or distance runner's ability to achieve greatness, is the VO2 max test, which assesses a body's ability to transport and use oxygen during exercise. This test is believed to describe your "ceiling" as an endurance athlete, the maximum ability you physically have to perform at an elite level.

Lauren got the worst score in the camp, even though in a prior race she had defeated most of the other women who were there.

Lauren looked at the numbers and thought she was examining the end of her dreams to be a state champion and future Olympian. Science said her body was overperforming already and that when she competed against elite athletes in the international arena, she just wouldn't possess the "hardware" to keep up.

Her coach, thank God, even though he was also a math teacher, dismissed the tests as "just science." He reminded Lauren that she had already run faster than almost every other girl who had tested better than her. "Life is not a math equation," he counseled his young runner. "Neither is running."

Lauren then called her dad and got a world-class pep talk. "You are a scrapper! A Fleshman! You can't measure the freaking heart of a Fleshman!"

Lauren kept running.

She went on to become a state champion and even a national high school runner-up. She not only earned a scholarship to Stanford, but her name is now inscribed on that competitive school's Wall of Champions. She is sponsored by Nike and has run professionally for more than a decade, including two victories as US National Champion in the 5000 meters.

Lauren remarked, "According to science, my 5K potential is 35 seconds slower than what I've actually clocked."[1]

Thirty-five seconds, in an elite 5K, is *huge*.

It's not that science isn't helpful; it's just not the end of the story, in physiology or in relationships. I use "science" all the time in premarital counseling, finding that the session when I take a couple through their Prepare and Enrich test results is often the most helpful and revealing session of all. The test tells couples where they are likely to stumble and serves as a general measure of overall compatibility.

As a tool, it can be very revealing:

"Oh, that's why she responds that way."

"That makes so much sense. Now I understand why he does that."

It also warns couples where hot-button items might threaten their relationship and suggests various points in the relationship that need to be addressed.

Some of you who are already married might all but flunk the Prepare and Enrich test (it's not set up to flunk anyone, but it certainly reveals levels of relational vulnerability). You might well be entirely incompatible in a scientific sense. But plenty of couples have risen above natural limitations to achieve more relationally than some objective test says might be possible. That's because the same God who is Lord over science is also Lord over the supernatural. It's possible to have supernatural science because our Creator God is King over both.

There's an inherent weakness in personality tests that sometimes gets ignored: the lie behind basing a marriage on compatibility more than mission is that we are never flash-frozen people. Spouses

—purpose driven leadership

continually change. Purpose—values that drive us—can be more concrete even than personality. Spiritual purpose and mission can overcome weaknesses in character because God redeems our characters; embracing the magnificent obsession can even overcome challenges in compatibility because, in the unity of the Spirit, you can join around a common mission.

The phrase "unity of the Spirit" might sound as weak as a Christian greeting card cliché, but it's a powerful scriptural truth that will lead to a more intimate union in your marriage. Two people united in God, filled with the Spirit, and jointly purposed to seek first His kingdom (Matt. 6:33) have a supernatural uniting presence in their relationship. It is more than enough to sustain them and to build a future on.

When God enters the equation—not as an add-on to the marriage, but as the foundation, the uniting force, the third presence, the empowering agent—He can *transform* us far above our natural limitations. Remember Jeremiah 31:4? "I will build you and you will be rebuilt" (NASB).

A truly sacred marriage points to a reality beyond our human limitations.

Your tests don't have to define you. Your compatibility doesn't have to be a ceiling over which your relationship can never rise. Your past hurts don't have to constitute the first steps in a journey toward divorce court. We worship, serve, and are empowered by a supernatural God who can lift us above our scientific limitations and create something special out of something very ordinary. These tests don't account for the power of a magnificent obsession.

Lauren hasn't (yet) won a gold medal at the Olympics or World Championships—but at the time of this writing she is one of the fastest American women alive and has had a career well worth celebrating. In the same way, you may never have the easiest or happiest marriage, but you can still build one well worth celebrating; just as important, you can build one that honors God, that provides a witness to the world, and that shelters your children. If your relationship is already "scientifically sound," adopting the vision of a magnificent obsession and choosing to pursue a more intimate union can still take your relationship to an entirely new level.

I want you to think about more than just the endgame, however. I want you to learn to surrender to the *process*. Building a more intimate union isn't easy—far from it! It's rewarding (few things in life are half as rewarding, in fact), but it takes more than a little effort to get there. The goal of this book isn't just to build marriages that stick it out with gritted teeth. It's not entitled *A Lifelong Marriage* but *A Lifelong Love* for a reason. Even when we face seemingly insurmountable challenges, marriage can build within us the all-important attitude of a conqueror. And that's what we are called by God to do.

Called to Conquer

Luo Wenyou, a man who enjoys restoring old cars, told a reporter, "However tired or hungry you are, when you hear the engine start after months of hard work, it's unbeatable, the happiest moment in life."[2]

Notice the principle here: bringing something back to life becomes more gratifying when it's particularly difficult to resurrect. I suspect that if Wenyou needed to spend just a short hour tinkering around in the garage in order to hear the motor turn over, he wouldn't call it "the happiest moment in life" but rather just another chore, like painting the fence.

Can we have the same attitude in marriage, recognizing that persevering and figuring out how to make a difficult challenge work can be enormously satisfying? Instead of looking at a spouse's addiction, attitude, broken past, or financial calamity only as dark tunnels that threaten to swallow us, can we also view them as challenges to face together, recognizing that when victory is won, the sound of a marriage finally working again will fill us with tremendous satisfaction? And that the process of overcoming these challenges actually took our intimacy to another level?

The challenges we face may not be cataclysmic: perhaps we just have to overcome the ordinary challenges of not becoming bored in our affection, lazy in our love, gradually taking each other for granted, and letting even our sexual intimacy fade into mere pleasantness. If we don't want that, can we see the challenge of restoring our relationship as an energizing opportunity?

One description of Christian identity that might help us comes from Paul in Romans 8:37: "In all these things we are more than conquerors through him who loved us" (ESV).

I'm currently working with a couple who may not make it. They went to an intensive marriage rescue weekend, but it didn't take. Then they came to me, and I arrived at the same conclusion as the rescue counselor did. One of them has an entrenched attitude that nothing will ever change, that it's always going to be the same, so why bother? This spouse isn't willing to leave the relationship but also isn't willing to live in it. That's a miserable place to be.

A defeatist attitude kills almost as many marriages as do affairs. If you are frustrated in any area of your marriage, will you choose to live by your past experience ("I've already tried, and it doesn't work") or will you choose to live by the truth of God's Word ("we are more than conquerors through him who loved us")? Do you view yourself as more than a conqueror or as one of the conquered? Will you be defeated, or a defeater? With God, the choice is yours.

The problem with not having a conquering attitude is that we're in warfare whether we recognize it or not. Spiritual, social, and personal forces are moving to tear all Christian couples apart. To embrace Jesus's call to "seek first His kingdom" is to enter into battle; Jesus's kingdom is hated by many, not least by Satan. Why, then, are we surprised when Satan and the forces of this world fight back against God's kingdom, beginning with His rule in our marriages? Why, indeed, are we surprised when our own sinful natures fight back against God's best for us, including the pursuit of an intimate union with our spouses?

To not be engaged in the warfare, to pretend our relationship, mission, and integrity aren't under attack, is tantamount to having a picnic in the middle of a battlefield and then being surprised when a grenade explodes under our table.

If you want to overcome the natural limitations of your marriage, you need to believe in the supernatural power of God to change. You need to have the attitude of being more than a conqueror. Otherwise, what hope do you have?

The Battles Before Us

Romans 8:37 does much more than tell us we should expect resistance; it goes on to gloriously proclaim something even greater than victory—that we are "more than conquerors." In other words, we are called to do more than just survive; we are called to rule, influence, and proclaim, including in our marriages. Those of you merely trying to keep your marriages alive have set the bar far too low.

That's why the subtitle of this book asks, what if marriage is about more than just staying together? It's not enough to survive; a lifelong love is all about thriving in a ministry-minded marriage that impacts others.

If you're looking at marriage only on a "scientific" basis, you'll put into play psychological practices and relational skills that may indeed be helpful—to an extent. I'm not talking these down *at all*—I'm just saying there is another element to account for. If you want to grow together beyond your natural limitations, consider adopting the following spiritual practices that can lift your marriage above its scientific limitations.

The first conquering to be done must be over our own sin: "[Sin] desires to have you, but you must rule over it" (Gen. 4:7). If we do not surrender to Holy Spirit–generated self-control—if we do not conquer our polluted thirsts—we cannot maintain the high level of marital intimacy God has designed us for. Sinful habits (gossip, pride, impatience, malice, resentment, and so forth) wreak havoc on marital oneness. The conquering, in other words, begins with ourselves.

Next, we seek to conquer evil in our homes; we assault the presence of others' sin with grace, mercy, loving confrontation, forgiveness, prayer, and a daily infusion of God's truth (which protects us from lies that bombard us). This last part is so important. We must conquer the lies that war against us, blunt our love, and lead us away from God's plan. That means—there is no substitute here—daily immersion in Scripture. Remember, we are transformed by the renewing of our minds (Rom. 12:1–2). Christianity is based on truth, which means, by definition, that Christian marriage is also based on truth, which means (are you still following me?) that we can't maintain intimacy with each other if we're not also maintaining intimacy with Scripture.

People who don't read the Bible on a daily basis must think Satan takes a day off. Good luck with that. The magnificent obsession is so foreign to my natural self that I need to be reminded of it every day. It takes me about twenty minutes to forget my highest ideals and start living selfishly again. Our short-term memory is a huge problem when it comes to the pursuit of holiness.

The world is lying to us every day about what will make us happy. I lie to myself every day about what will make me happy. I have to hear from God what is truly true lest I pour all my energies into pursuing something that can never satisfy. The one place where I know I will never be lied to is when I safely walk in the meadow of God's Word. No errors exist there; no enemies or tricks will ever be hidden in the pages of God's revelation. I can rest in the refreshing truth that gives life and wholeness.

The final step to becoming more than a conqueror is to conquer evil in the world. Saved from sin, more than conquerors at home, victors over the lies that assault us, we can go out and fight on behalf of other couples and other families. This is the missional aspect of God's plan for marriage.

Let's not settle for less. We aren't described as conquerors. We are called "more than conquerors." Addicts, God wants more from you than to merely defeat your bad habits. He wants you to be more than a conqueror—He would have you conquer yourself so that you can conquer for others.

Couples on the verge of breaking up: God wants more of you than to merely hold on and stay together. He wants to do more than merely save your marriage. He would have you learn the lessons you must learn, conquer in your home, and then become a couple advocate for other couples who are drowning in defeat, starving for joy, thirsting for oneness.

Dream together: "If we get through this, how do you think God might use us?"

The journey to a more intimate union begins with understanding that business as usual means drifting apart. There's a war going on—a war that launches loneliness, apathy, and isolation against the God-given call to intimacy, passion, and community.

Yes, there is fierce resistance. Yes, it would feel so much easier to just disengage. So what will sustain us? Not our own wisdom, and certainly not our own power or goodness. We are more than conquerors, Paul tells us, *through him who loved us.* When we truly experience, understand, rest in, and relish the love that is poured out on us—a knowledge and understanding dependent on divine revelation (Eph. 3:14–18)—we have hope because we know God loves us, has our backs, will lift us up, and can't be defeated. "I have loved you with an everlasting love; therefore I have drawn you with lovingkindness. Again I will build you and you will be rebuilt" (Jer. 31:3–4 NASB).

It is such a trap to fall into defeated thinking: *I can't be happy; my wife is a hopeless alcoholic. My husband will never get away from his game console. I can't make it another day in this marriage; I just can't. My wife and I will never understand each other; we just won't. We're too incompatible.*

Scripture calls us to rise up and say, "This day, in His name, I conquer!"

This might sound hopelessly hokey to some of you, but for others, it really could be a powerful start-the-day battle cry. We know that wars can be long, that battles sometimes involve momentary setbacks, but we take each day as a new opportunity to conquer, to gain new ground, to faithfully advance His kingdom. "This day, in His name, I conquer! Yesterday, I might have had my teeth kicked in, but this day, I conquer!"

Here's the reality: There are *supposed* to be challenges in your life and your marriage. You're engaged in spiritual warfare! Soldiers aren't surprised when the enemy shoots at them or lays a trap.

God's work in this world is far from done. That's why we're here—to keep fighting these battles. That's why we are being filled with God's Spirit—to rise up and conquer in His name.

Remember the story of the Mennonites in Belize? It's not what we're given; it's what we do with it. "This day, in His name, I conquer!" Are you ready to defeat rather than be defeated?

Now let's get into the relational aspects of how two people can grow ever more in love instead of regularly growing in disappointment.

Building a Lifelong Love

1. On a scale of one to ten, with one being not compatible at all and ten being perfectly compatible in every way, how would you rate you and your spouse?

2. Discuss the value and the limitations of compatibility tests for believers.

3. What are the dangers of two compatible spouses living without a sense of mission? How can two less compatible spouses use spiritual mission and a reliance on God to have hope that they can enjoy a fruitful and fulfilling marriage?

4. Do you live with the awareness that spiritual warfare is happening in your marriage? How might this affect the way you and your partner relate to each other?

5. Five years from now, if someone were to describe you and your spouse as "more than conquerors," what would they likely be referring to? What can the two of you begin doing today to perhaps hear someone say that to you in the future?

Our conquering God, with You as our general, we know there is no war that can't be won. Thank You for promising to be with us every moment of every battle. You are the God who created us, and You are the God who promises to recreate us, so we ask You to overcome any natural hindrances to our relationship and instead lay a supernatural pathway whereby the two of us can become one in every sense of the word. We put our hope not in any gimmicks or even in human effort but in Your promise, Your provision, Your wisdom, and Your Spirit. In Jesus's name, amen.

Richard
Fran
Demas
Alan
Kelly
Phill
Diane
Vic
Danny
Donna

10

Artificial Intimacy

Popular thinking assumes good marriages are "discovered"—you meet the right person, and it's like planting a tree seedling. At first, you water it and weed around it, you might even stake it, but after a year or two, the tree just grows. Occasionally, you might want to keep watering it if you live in a particularly dry climate, but for the most part, you can ignore it and still watch it grow.

That's how most couples live. They'll talk about their pasts when they first meet, get engaged, go through premarital counseling, but after the wedding, the marriage is supposed to somehow "finish itself" just by the fact that it exists.

That's not an accurate expectation of marriage. Intimate marriage is more like building a brick house. If you get a good start, even laying half the bricks, and then stop building, the house won't finish itself. In fact, the reality is worse: an unfinished house, left out in the weather, deteriorates. The same is true of marriage. If we aren't dedicated to saying "I do" every day *after* the wedding, then, relationally speaking, that's a day lost. Some couples who signed their wedding licenses twenty-five years ago have actually only been working on their marriages for about six months. They quit moving toward each other long ago. Long-term marital intimacy requires accepting this truth: *to stop giving yourself to your spouse is to spiritually divorce them*.

Every season of life tempts us to stop building our marriages. We get lost fighting lesser battles. If we asked couples on their wedding day, "Are you going to be more concerned about how big your office is than how intimate your marriage is?" or "Do you care more about how impressed people are by your house than how well the two of you relate to each other as a couple?" or "Do you think you'll find satisfaction in life by being respected for what you do while being miserable at home?" I think most would say no. But the way they live, the priorities they set, and what they give their time and energy to, is often exactly the opposite.

Rather than grow together in true intimacy, far too many couples exist only on what I call "artificial intimacy." They've never intentionally built intimacy but rather were trapped by an infatuation that felt like it fell from heaven. They never had to work at it; it just was. Once it died, their intimacy died with it. An artificial intimacy can be sustained for a time by the common events of life, but usually it comes to a huge crash as soon as the couple enters the empty-nest years if true intimacy hasn't replaced it.

Let's look at how artificial intimacy begins, how it is temporarily sustained, and then how couples who believe they have been gripped by it can learn to grow into true intimacy.

In the Beginning

Artificial intimacy begins with the onset of infatuation, a "grab your brains with a vengeance" neurochemical reaction that makes you virtually blind to your partner's faults. Infatuation is notoriously short-lived, with a shelf life of about twelve to eighteen months, but it's intense. It's also artificial, in that it creates an idealization of the one you love. You focus on strengths (many of which might be imaginary) and ignore weaknesses (many of which are readily apparent to outside observers). You idealize this person to make them the kind of person you *want* them to be. It's not genuine intimacy, but it feels real and is enough to lead many couples into marriage. At this point you are relating to an idealized, fictional version of a man or woman, not that person's authentic self.

In addition to infatuation, your relationship compatibility is also enhanced artificially via initial sexual chemistry, which tends to be very strong. When infatuation and sexual chemistry coexist, incompatibility barely even registers. You feel crazy about each other, you can barely keep your hands off each other—how could you *not* have an amazing marriage? You don't even have to do anything to sustain your desire for each other; just being alive makes you feel compatible. And so, on primarily this basis, the couple decides to get married.

When Spring Turns to Summer

When a couple sets a date for the wedding, even though the initial artificial intimacy may be on the decline (unless they're getting married within the first six to eight months of meeting), planning the ceremony gives them something in common and keeps them going. They plan it, talk about it, and divide up tasks to make it happen. This is intimacy of a sort, but it's a superficial intimacy, the intimacy of coworkers, not life mates. Still, in the throes of infatuation and high sexual chemistry, it feels like true intimacy and continues to sustain the relationship. They have a huge goal—the wedding day—and the anticipation of that day and their new life together can feel more real than the life they are already living.

This dynamic explains why I implore engaged couples to set strict ground rules that three days out of the week they will not talk about the wedding ceremony—period. It is silly to give so much focus to a ceremony lasting less than an hour while neglecting the cultivation of a lifelong relationship. If the couple doesn't do this, the honeymoon can hit them pretty hard. They'll be thrilled the ceremony is over, enjoy the sexual consummation, and then spend the first few days talking about what went right at the wedding, what went wrong, who was there, who wasn't there, and so on. About the third or fourth day of the honeymoon, the thirty-minute ceremony and two-hour reception will be talked to death. If they have put true relational intimacy on hold, once the false intimacy of ceremony planning has been discussed ad nauseam, the couple is likely to fall into an awkward and even terrifying silence. When you've been living for something that is now past, you're like a five-year-old child on December 26. The surprise is over, and reality isn't quite as enchanting. (Do you realize it's not all that uncommon for wives to fight back tears during their honeymoon?)

Once the couple gets back from the honeymoon, they start setting up a home by moving into a new apartment or neighborhood and trying to join two lives. That also joins them in a common task and gives them something to talk about. What color should we paint the bedroom? Do you think we'll be here long enough to bother with planting trees outside? Where's our new favorite coffee shop?

As life moves on, just when things could get boring again, the couple is likely to start raising kids. That's a big thing to have in common and requires a lot of communication. You go to childbirth classes, you build a nursery, you raise the kids, and then you have to communicate to get the kids to the right places. You share your kids' failures and successes until you start to fight about them.

That's when you find out how much intimacy you really have.

At the start of the relationship it was just infatuation and sexual chemistry. Then it was the joint task of planning a ceremony. Then, setting up a home. After that, raising kids. In days past, these life events could take marriages to the doorstep of death, but modern couples (who tend to have fewer children) can blow through these stages of life in two and a half decades, often leaving another thirty years or more of marriage to follow. That's a long time to be lonely and to live with a familiar-looking stranger. If you haven't consciously built true intimacy, the relationship is going to be seriously threatened.

Some couples have to wake up to the reality that they've been living relationally on shared tasks, not shared intimacy, which is built by praying together, sharing your dreams, carrying each other's burdens, and building that all-important empathy for each other. Instead, they're teammates, not spouses, and when you're merely teammates and the season is over, what do teammates do? They go their own ways.

This in part explains why so many couples suddenly declare incompatibility even though they obviously once thought they had found their perfect match in each other and have lived together for more than two decades. They've simply come to the end of this false compatibility and realize they have very little common ground with which to face the rest of their life together. Sadly, they don't realize it's possible to rebuild the marriage on spiritual compatibility and by choosing empathy and intimacy (we discussed the former in the first section, and are about to get into the latter in this section).

When a couple gets divorced and each individual starts over with someone else, the second relationship initially feels more fulfilling than the first because, once again, it's existing on artificial intimacy: infatuation and sexual chemistry retake their place on center stage, and the two infatuated lovers enter the relationship-building practice of sharing past histories, planning a ceremony, and setting up a new life together. But the same dynamics will bring this affection to an end as well if the couple doesn't consciously build true intimacy.

Making a Marriage

One of the main messages of my writing and speaking career on marriage has been this: a good marriage isn't something you find; it's something you make, and you have to keep on making it. Just as importantly (and herein lies the hope), you can also begin remaking it at any stage.

If you wake up to the sobering reality that you've existed on artificial intimacy, the good news is that there's a relatively easy, though not quick, fix: you can begin now to build true intimacy. It is much better for everyone involved if, instead of seeking a divorce and building yet another relationship on artificial intimacy, the couple chooses to begin building true intimacy, with God as the center of the relationship.

If you believe a good marriage is something you find, and the one you've found isn't working, you can't fix that—you simply ended up with the wrong person and the only logical solution is divorce. If you believe a good marriage is something you make, and it's not working, you can choose to remake it, to do something different, to build it up in a different way.

As a Christian, I believe we are so self-centered that we need to be transformed with God's Spirit working within us to give us the full capacity to know true empathy, a willingness to sacrifice, and the ability to overcome the petty sins that destroy affection and create bitterness. That's just another way of saying that building and sustaining true intimacy require nothing less than God's direct intervention through His Holy Spirit. It's no good just starting over with another sinner who simply sins in different ways, because eventually I'll grow just as weary with the second wife's sins as I did with my first wife's sins. How much better to attack the sin and grow in the grace of forgiveness than to live on a carousel of ever-changing spouses.

True intimacy is thus built via thoughtful, God-empowered perseverance: the commitment to keep doing small things that feed relational intimacy, in their proper priority. As a married couple, we persistently communicate; there is no relationship without communication. We don't let bitterness grow. We keep caring enough to resolve our differences, and we go to God to forgive each other's weaknesses. We reserve time for each other. We make memories between the two of us—this is an intentional pursuit of deciding to do mutually enjoyable things together, without the kids. We remain the best of friends, and alarms go off if anyone else begins to feel closer or more desirable to us than our spouse. We keep praying for each other. We learn to laugh together, and we play together, work together, and cry together. If there's not a physical reason why sex stops or becomes less frequent, we find out why our intimacy is on the wane and address it.

If we stop doing the things that sustain marital intimacy, the relationship withers and dies. What's so sad is that when couples get to the end of artificial intimacy, they often blame it on the person instead of the relationship. They say, "I must have married the wrong person" instead of "We haven't nurtured the relationship." This is tantamount to paying an A-list architect to design a house, quit building it halfway through, and then saying, "This is just a defective plan; water comes right through the hole in our roof!" The problem isn't with the architect; the problem is with the builders who didn't finish the job.

Ever notice how particular God was with the right way to build His temple? He laid out exact specifications for everything from the length and height of every room to the doorjambs to the fixtures and even how everything should be decorated. Our marriages can be "temples"—Jesus said where two or more people come together in His name, there He is. Paul teaches us, "Do you not know that you are a temple of God and that the Spirit of God dwells in you?" (1 Cor. 3:16 NASB). God is into building, and He'll help us build a "marriage-temple" if we invite Him to. You think He's reluctant to help construct another monument to His glory, another outpost for His kingdom work?

A glorious temple doesn't just happen, though. God could have spoken the temple into existence, but He chose to use builders. He gave very specific instructions, but those instructions required obedience, effort, and initiative.

Intimacy is something we can choose to build and even rebuild if it has been lost. If two people want to rekindle their love, by God's grace they can, just by doing the things couples do. Intimacy isn't something you "have" or "don't have" as much as it is something you *choose*.

The next chapter will provide a marital road map of sorts—it lists the most common stages of marriage in which couples stop growing together. Knowing they exist can help us be more intentional in our pursuit of oneness.

Building a Lifelong Love

1. If you were to evaluate your marriage on the basis of <u>artificial intimacy and true intimacy</u>, where would you place your relationship?

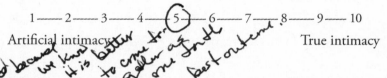

1 —— 2 —— 3 —— 4 —— 5 —— 6 —— 7 —— 8 —— 9 —— 10
Artificial intimacy   True intimacy

[handwritten: More connected because we know it is better to come to gather at the Inth one best outcome]

2. Do you feel more connected as a couple and more involved in each other's lives now than you did on your wedding day, or in some ways do you feel further apart? Why do you think that is so?

3. Where do you fall on the following spectrum?

1 —— 2 —— 3 —— 4 —— 5 —— 6 —— 7 —— 8 —— 9 —— 10
Expected marriage   Worked to build marriage
to largely grow on its own

4. What one thing can you and your spouse do in the coming weeks (or you can do on your own if your spouse has checked out) to begin building or rebuilding true intimacy?

Father, we know You desire us to be an intimate couple, enjoying and modeling true intimacy. We once were so satisfied with something that wasn't even real. Give us a new thirst for authentic intimate union. Thank You for letting us grow bored with what was artificial and for giving us souls that will not easily settle for something that is less than best. We recognize any current sense of disconnect as a sign that, perhaps, we have let other things come in the way of truly growing together. We pray that You will help us to make better choices so that, one year from now, we will be living in a substantially different and more intimate marriage, enough so that even family members and friends will recognize it. In Jesus's name, amen.

Kelly
Phil
Richard
Denise
Fran
Alan
Dion
Vic
Danny
Donnie

11

Pushing Past the Power Shifts

Just as you see momentum swinging wildly from one basketball team to another, in marriage, "relational power" can shift from spouse to spouse. I call these movements "power shifts."

By "power," I'm referring to one spouse gaining the upper hand relationally. One partner feels less secure or more invested in the relationship than the other one, which gives the more secure partner more "power." If you feel like you're more into the marriage than your spouse is, it will feel like your spouse has more power, because he or she doesn't care as much as you do (or at least, your spouse doesn't seem to care as much and certainly seems to feel more secure). This often shifts through the years.

The net effect of power shifts is loneliness—the opposite of intimacy. Instead of two people moving toward each other, it feels like one is running after the other, and the other (the one with the power) won't wait up. Instead of the marriage flourishing as an intimate union, it becomes a desperate chase, and few things make someone feel lonelier than chasing after someone else.

Loneliness in marriage is especially painful. That's why we need to know the typical power shifts so that we can grow through them instead of having our intimacy buried in them. Power shifts, if not recognized or handled maturely, usually give birth to bitterness and resentment. Then, when the power shifts back to us, out of our bitterness, we use it as a weapon and do even further damage to the relationship.

Here's what's key: every power shift I'm going to mention also has the potential to build intimacy if it is properly navigated with empathy, prayer, conversation, worship, and service. I'll talk about where partners often go wrong, but that's only to help us choose to do what's right by comparison. We can walk out of each season closer and more intimate if we choose to.

For the sake of brevity, I'm going to gender stereotype a bit; please understand I'm *well aware* that the gender roles I'm discussing are often reversed. If I have to keep qualifying myself, saying "or her" every time I say "him," we'll both get bored, so please take no offense.

I Want You

"It's going to be a short reception."

"Okay."

"No. I mean, *really* short."

Brent was thirty-one when he got married, and a virgin. He couldn't wait to *not* be a virgin. So when his wife agreed to marry him at two on a Saturday, he fully expected to no longer be a virgin by, say, six that evening.

His wife laughed, appreciated his life of faithfulness, and ultimately agreed to leave the reception barely an hour after it had begun.

The only problem was, they got to the luxury hotel before turndown service began. Neither thought twice about it until, just moments before Brent could achieve his goal, there was a persistent and loud knock on the door:

"Turndown service! Housekeeping!"

"You have *got* to be kidding me!" Brent exclaimed.

Then the door started opening.

"Don't worry. I've got this," his wife said, climbing naked out of bed, wrapping a towel around the most salient parts of her body, and trying to appear as normal as possible when she explained that, even though it was 5:45 p.m., they really didn't want to be disturbed, and that, yes, she prefers to wear a towel in the early evening, thank you very much.

I've done weddings for many guys who are "chomping at the bit." The sexual energy (assuming they are not already sleeping with their fiancées) keeps them laser focused on their wives-to-be. They are solicitous. They are attentive. They are kind. The soon-to-be-wives realize they have a lot of power in the relationship. It's comforting and safe and fulfilling.

Unfortunately, there's something about the male psyche where, after the wedding, we naturally think, *I've got the girl;*

what's the next challenge? The sexual relationship is very satisfying, but now that the itch is being regularly scratched, we suddenly become obsessed with succeeding at work, becoming a scratch golfer, rebuilding a car, moving up in rankings on a video game, and so forth. The young wife understandably feels aggrieved: "I used to be number one in his life, and now I'm priority number five or six?"

Power has shifted back to the guy. The wife feels she is now more into the relationship than her husband is, and it hurts. It's scary. She has committed her life (her *entire life*!) to this man, making her feel vulnerable, but she did so under different circumstances. Her husband, once so thoughtful and attentive, now seems like a completely different man, much less solicitous, much less into her. Who wants to face a lifetime of trying to compete for your husband's attention with all the crass things of this world that feed a man's ego?

Men (or women, if you do this), we can do a lot of damage to our spouses' esteem and our marital intimacy when we present one front while dating and another front after the wedding, moving from being so invested in our partners and the relationship to only appearing somewhat interested, at best. The prior intensity of our affection and interest will make the current apathy all the more painful. If you've already fallen into this trap, an apology (even ten years or more after the fact) never hurts. We have to own up to an immature response to having been led primarily by sexual chemistry (it can be much more than this, of course, but remember, I'm stereotyping). Our sexual desire made us attentive, but our desire and attention were a means, not an end. We didn't cherish our wives exclusively; we cherished what our (preferably naked) wives had to offer.

This is why I'll often tell guys in premarital counseling, "Make sure you step up your romance *after* the wedding."

One thing I did was to buy ten gifts for Lisa and bring them on our honeymoon. The first evening, I put all the wrapped gifts on a table and said, "You can open one every night and one in the morning." They weren't expensive—I had virtually no money and no assets other than a ten-year-old Ford Maverick Grabber—but it was a statement that I wanted to show Lisa my appreciation *after* she had made the commitment, not just before.

When the husband gets sloppy here, all too often he sets himself up to be the loser in the next power shift—baby infatuation.

A Little Affair

"The arrival of my son had completely altered my relationship with my husband. Though I certainly expected my marriage to change once we had children, I was not prepared for a complete loss of intimacy. We had been a tight-knit team, albeit a motley one, but now we were satellites in separate orbits, crossing paths only when it came to our child. My friends with kids assured me that the situation was natural and would right itself over time, after the shock of our new addition wore off. One friend, a mom of three, went beyond that: 'You can't expect to feel the same way about your husband now. Your relationship needs to change so your son can be your focus. Our brains are wired so our kids can come first. It's an evolutionary thing.'"[1]

Well, that "evolutionary thing" didn't work so well for the mother-author in question. She and her husband eventually got a divorce, and how well did that divorce serve the kids whom she was counseled to focus on first?

I don't mean to slam anyone here—I'm just pointing out that beliefs have consequences. We have to fight to *not* let the kids come first and thus destroy the stability of our kids' home—even when they're babies. The default mode seems to always be to put each other last, but the consequences of doing so end up harming our children far more than they'd suffer if we left them with Grandma for a regular date-night getaway.

Women often hate it when their husbands make the not-uncommon charge that it feels like they're having "affairs" with their firstborn children. There's some neurological support for this, however. When a mother is nursing her child, oxytocin is flooding her brain (a neuropeptide that results in feelings of warmth and affection) and she is bonding and rebonding in the most powerful of God-created ways. For some women, it can be just as strong as an infatuation, though it's different from a romantic infatuation.

In fact, a woman doesn't even have to nurse the baby to get this neurologic effect. All she has to do is *smell* the baby. A German study found that the mere odor of a newborn baby activates the neurological reward circuit in mothers (not just women, mind you, but women who are mothers). Two similar neurological experiences would be the pleasure you get when beginning to eat when you're really hungry and the craving an addict feels when first getting his drug—the same part of the brain fires up in all three instances. In other words, men, your wife, if she's a mom, has the same neurological response to smelling a baby as you do to downing that hamburger at the turn during a round of golf.[2]

Which explains why some wives, six or seven weeks after the child has been born, respond to the husband's suggestion that they leave the baby with someone else just to get away, with, "Why would I leave *my baby* to spend time alone with *you?*" No, she won't actually say that, but the horror on her face when just the idea is presented tells her husband all he needs to know.

You see, she's perhaps felt slighted ever since the wedding. Her man as a fiancé was so into her, but then, when he became a husband, he pulled back. She tried and tried to get his attention back to where it was, and she failed. Now she has a baby, someone with whom she is experiencing that level of intimacy she has longed for all her life. This baby is so focused on her—he even cries when someone else dares hold him—and she's been so thirsty for appreciation and intimacy that it's understandable to a certain degree that she'd become imbalanced. She thinks the baby will always be this focused on her because she is blissfully unaware of God's divine remedy for baby infatuation (it's called adolescence, but that's a decade away).

Meanwhile, the husband eventually realizes he's "lost" his wife. She speaks tenderly to the baby in a way that she hasn't spoken to him in months, if not years. If the baby cries, the husband stops existing. They could be in the middle of making love, but that doesn't matter—the baby comes first. The power has shifted back to the wife. And the wife can do a lot of harm to her marriage if, ruled by those strong maternal feelings, she succumbs to the trap of becoming a mom first and a wife second.

Of course, it's not just women who fall into this. When the men do it, the couple is set up to experience what I call "baby bouncing."

Baby Bouncing

Francine ultimately grieved when her husband, Jacques, fell madly in love with their firstborn child, Eliane. That might sound odd; wouldn't a mother love the fact that her husband so adored her daughter?

Well, we're human. Francine explained it this way: "I had loved and admired Jacques since I was 18. Our meeting had been providential and had changed our lives completely. The arrival of our baby ... seemed to complicate things. Jacques only had eyes for her, she was his little angel. I was no longer the only one he loved. I felt frustrated, as if something had been taken away from me."[3]

Although Francine isn't proud of this, you can kind of see it, can't you? This man she had loved all her adult life suddenly seemed to be pouring his affection out on someone he seemed to love more than her. Even though that someone was her daughter, it still hurt. And when we hurt, we sometimes do hurtful things.

In this case, Francine eventually compensated by pouring out her love on second-born Suzanne, who arrived four years later.

Jacques didn't seem to love Suzanne as much as he did Eliane, so Francine felt justified in compensating by loving Suzanne more than Eliane. Now she had an ally in her war of hurt against Jacques. Finally, power had been balanced: it was two against two, Francine and Suzanne together suffering the favored-union status of Jacques and Eliane. Without knowing why or even seeming to choose to do so, Francine found herself constantly critical of Eliane, making her feel as if she could do no right while Suzanne could do no wrong.

The issue, of course, wasn't Eliane or Suzanne. The issue was spurned love in the marriage being played out through the kids, or "baby bouncing"—compensating for favored status of one child by favoring another. The children become pawns in the marital shifts of power and affection.

One fateful week, Jacques and Francine went on vacation and took the leisure time not only to pray but also to listen to God—I mean, *really* listen. By inviting God to speak into their lives, the couple sensed Him pointing out the dark dynamics of why Francine felt bitter toward Eliane and why she favored Suzanne. Not only did the recognition and resulting confession restore Jacques and Francine's love, but Francine took it one step further and apologized to Eliane, who said, "At last you've admitted it. You did love Suzanne more than me. I knew it!" Eliane gave her a big hug, and deep healing began. That might seem like an awkward conversation—a parent admitting that—but what other choice was there? Eliane knew it whether Francine admitted it or not. Best to confess, explain it, and use it as a pathway to grow and as a demonstration of God's redeeming work.

When a marriage gets sick, the family gets sick. To stop building your marriage for the sake of your children is like leaving them out in the rain while you cook their dinner. Don't bounce marital dysfunction from child to child. Don't let the dynamics of your marriage cause you to enlist your children in a covert war against your spouse (it's not just divorced spouses who pit their children against each other). If you feel neglected, tell each other. If you believe you've lost your spouse's heart, don't ever think you can compensate by trying to gain control of your child's heart. Our children aren't pawns; they're not to be used to soothe the aches in our marriages. They're to be cherished, supported, nurtured, trained, and launched into their own life of love.

Talk to each other. Listen to God. Seek counsel. Resolve that the child-rearing years will create memories and partnership and shared purpose instead of bitterness, resentment, and alienation.

Checking Out

The next power shift often occurs right here. If the husband realizes he has lost his wife to the kids (or to the kids and her career, or to his wife's parents, who now need extra care, or even, at times, to the family pet), he is likely to pursue his ego needs in another arena. One thing I've learned about men: if we don't think we can win, we usually won't even compete; we just start focusing elsewhere. If we can't find respect at home, we'll search for it outside the home. It might be at work, on a video game, at the golf course, or in a deer blind. But we'll stray however far we must to get some semblance of respect, even if the arena of that respect is microscopic.

This becomes a relational cancer when the other spouse responds in kind: "Okay, it's clear he has checked out. That reinforces my decision to refocus on the kids, because he's not. He just sits there in front of his video games. Someone has to be the adult!" "Checking out" is usually cyclical—each partner's actions reinforce the other's—pushing the couple further and further apart.

Resentment, like some forms of cancer, is patient. It may exist in the relational bloodstream for a decade or more before showing any symptoms. The marriage gets colder and colder as the relationship gets sicker and sicker, but it's a slow descent, so the couple gradually gets used to the notion of becoming strangers who share the same bed.

This is a prime season for affairs, a lapse into addictions, or any other unhealthy coping mechanism. Lonely Christians do things they never could have imagined doing when they weren't lonely. And lonely Christians might even bring up the *d* word (divorce) when the kids leave home and there isn't anything holding the two of them together anymore.

One sign of checking out is that your social circles are becoming distinct and separate. Social science has revealed that many cases of divorce are caused not by an affair or abuse, but rather by the slow, gradual loss of the couple's social circle. As both partners find new social circles (whether at work, online, or at parent-teacher clubs), their shared social circle as a couple begins to fade into two separate circles. This makes divorce easier and more fathomable to conceive because each partner already belongs somewhere else and they have less of a home to lose.

If you want to fireproof your marriage, ensure that you do the opposite of "checking out," and instead do everything in your power to "check in" to your partner's social circle. If someone is important to your spouse, he or she needs to become important to you. Modern work schedules and online communities mean that it is inevitable spouses will build relationships outside of each other, but there should be no *significant* relationship that the other spouse isn't aware of and at least a part of (at minimum, by talking about it).

"Checking out" is the beginning of the end; "checking in" is the journey toward intimacy and joy.

Empty House, Empty Hearts

"This is the way to watch baseball!"

Graham (my son, who at the time was in college) and I were in sports heaven, sitting in the Diamond Club at a Houston Astros game, spitting distance (literally) from the catcher. My friend Skip, who provided the tickets, just smiled.

Skip is about fifteen years older than me, and I've found him to be a helpful source with whom to discuss common family issues that are new to me. My youngest daughter, Kelsey, was just weeks away from entering her first year in college at the time, so I asked Skip what I could expect in my marriage now that Lisa and I were about to become empty nesters. Lisa had been enormously involved in our kids' lives. She didn't want or have a career outside the home, and now life was about to change in a drastic way.

"She's going to need more affirmation than you can imagine," Skip told me. Graham's jaw dropped opened as he listened, and we just looked at each other. We had both found that as much as we had tried to encourage Lisa lately, it wasn't enough. Skip was explaining why.

"Everything she used to get her esteem from is now gone, in a sense, and she's got to find a new life. That's scary. You're going to have to be more attentive than ever and keep building her up."

This isn't true just for wives becoming empty nesters but also for wives or husbands who are entering retirement. When something has defined you for most of your adult life and that something has been taken away, doesn't it make sense that the marriage will take on some new stress? This is an invitation to step up marital intimacy, to become more engaged as a couple, to see it as an opportunity instead of a burden.

Most life events are like that—they are opportunities to make deposits in our marriages by investing in our spouses' emotional well-being, or they become failed tests that lead to withdrawal when we don't step up and we pretend that nothing has changed. We have to see that doing the same thing when the situation has changed could be considered an act of cruelty. If my wife is swimming in a lake, laughing and bobbing up and down, I can just watch her from afar and smile. If she's suddenly tired, now screaming and struggling to stay afloat, and I do nothing, that's unspeakably cruel.

The challenge is that emotional needs are rarely so obvious as someone drowning in a lake. Maybe our spouses are ashamed to admit their needs; maybe they're afraid that if they raise the issue it'll scare us off or that we won't step up. Sometimes pushing past the power shifts is about unilaterally stepping up when our spouses need us to, even without being asked, even if it means we have to study them to figure out what they truly need.

If your husband or wife retires and suddenly starts hanging around you more, you can have one of two responses: "Where were you the last thirty years?" or "We've kind of become strangers, haven't we? Well, let's see how we can regrow our relationship." The window is rather small, a few months at best. You're going to set a new pattern sooner rather than later. You'll either learn to stay apart even though your schedules don't demand it, or you'll learn how to become a more intimate couple.

There's one more power shift I need to mention, though I wish I didn't have to. It is one that many men, in particular, don't face very well.

See You Later

I've looked into the faces of more women than I can bear as they told me of how they were diagnosed with multiple sclerosis, or cancer, or Parkinson's, and the husband decided to take the medical diagnosis as an "escape clause" to find a woman who wasn't "broken." One medical doctor said that the number is actually around 70 percent—that seven out of ten men, upon hearing of a wife's cataclysmic medical diagnosis, leave the marriage.

I'm always shocked at two things when I hear these stories: the stoicism and strength of the women telling me their stories, and the unashamedly selfish, cruel response of the men. I know—there are no doubt male readers who have been on the other side, so please, don't feel the need to email me in protest. I have stated that I'm dealing in stereotypes, and I'm giving you your due right here. On the whole, it seems to be far more common for the husbands to leave.

One man who challenges me to this day with his entirely different response is Dr. Robertson McQuilkin, past president of Columbia Bible College and Seminary (now Columbia International University) from 1968 to 1990. There was a time when Dr. McQuilkin and his wife, Muriel, were a "power couple" in Christian circles, often headlining conferences. That all changed when a doctor at Duke confirmed that Muriel had Alzheimer's.

Because the McQuilkins were a popular couple, Robertson received every kind of legitimate and illegitimate advice you could imagine as to what would cure his wife, so he finally told everyone to please just stop with the suggestions. In his words, "We would trust the Lord to work a miracle in Muriel if he so desired or work a miracle in me if he didn't."[4]

This is such a stellar statement from a husband: "Lord, I pray You will do a physical miracle in my wife, but if You choose not to, then work a spiritual miracle in me so that I can love her well until the end."

And that's what he did. Muriel loved art, so Robertson took her to the Tate galleries in London, where some of Muriel's favorite works were kept. Unfortunately, the disease had advanced to such a state that Muriel already had good days and bad days, and this was not a good day. Robertson recounted, "A great sadness swept over me as I watched her rush through the gallery with never a glance at the masterworks she had loved so long." Robertson grieved that, in one sense, part of his wife was already gone.

On the flight to London, Robertson had faced the embarrassing necessity of following his wife into the airplane's cubicle toilet. He saw the smirks around him, and he knew what some were thinking: *Aren't you a little old to be joining the mile-high club?* Yet Robertson followed her anyway, because "I knew what they didn't; if she ever got the door shut—unlikely as that might be—she never could have gotten it open again."

At the airport on their way home, while waiting for their flight to leave, Muriel got restless. Robertson had learned that in such circumstances it was best to just let her roam, so he trailed behind her, carrying their bags, and sat when Muriel wanted to sit, and then got up and followed her again when she wanted to walk. Sometimes he practically had to jog, still toting those bags, trying to keep up.

Muriel eventually sat down across from a businesswoman whose dress and demeanor screamed power, influence, and success, working diligently on her laptop. Muriel kept up with her ADD-like fidgeting, but she always returned to this same seat across from the businesswoman. Every time, Robertson followed

Muriel to make sure she was okay. Finally, after they had returned from yet another short jaunt to the same seat, the businesswoman quietly spoke. No one else was around, so Robertson assumed she was talking to him. "Pardon?" he asked.

"Oh," she said, slightly embarrassed, "I was just asking myself, 'Will I ever find a man to love me like that?'"

Men, think about this: a successful businesswoman who had achieved what so many say they desire—affluence, power, purpose, position, influence—was literally envious of an Alzheimer's patient, wondering if a man would ever love her as Robertson loved Muriel. It's a stunning admission of our passionate yearning to be loved, even when everything else in life seems to be going so well. I'm not saying this woman would have traded places with Muriel. Of course not. Just that there was a part of her that, even in the face of her success, wondered what such love really felt like. There was a novel behind her answer, if anyone cared to explore it.

For her part, Muriel kept on loving Robertson as well, as best she could. That's what led to his resignation. During the latter days of Robertson's college presidency, Muriel would chase after him, sometimes as many as ten times a day, speed walking on her way to his office. Sometimes she lost her way, but she kept walking anyway, desperate to find the one person with whom she felt at home. One night, as Robertson helped Muriel undress, he recoiled at the sight of her bloody feet. Earlier in the day, she had so panicked to get out of the house to find him that she had neglected to put on her shoes and had ripped much of the skin off the bottom of her feet.

That was it for Robertson. He decided to lay aside the power of his position, the prestige of his employment, the intellectual stimulation of the college environment to which he had dedicated his life and to stay home with his wife. In a farewell address, he explained that it wasn't, in the end, all that hard: "The decision to come to Columbia was the most difficult I have had to make; the decision to leave 22 years later, though painful, was one of the easiest. The decision was made, in a way, 42 years ago when I promised to care for Muriel 'in sickness and in health ... till death do us part.'"

Now a stay-at-home husband, Robertson had time to read things he wouldn't have read before, such as a national advice columnist. He was puzzled by how often people wrote in, wanting to leave their marriages because the relationships weren't meeting their "needs." The columnist's answers were predictable as she laid out common-sense reasons to end a marriage. Robertson said, "There is an eerie irrelevance to every one of those criteria for me." Which one of his needs could Muriel meet now?

Instead of lecturing on the book of Acts, Robertson found himself cleaning up his wife after her more frequent bathroom accidents. He was listening to a popular radio preacher one time while doing so, and the preacher's dulcet voice challenged, "Men! Are you at home? Really at home?"

With feces on his hands, Robertson found himself smiling. "Yeah, Chuck, I'm really at home. Trust me. I'm *really* at home."

Robertson's doctor was deeply moved by the care this seminary president gave to his wife, and that's when he told him that seven out of ten American men leave their marriages when their wives get catastrophic medical diagnoses.

Robertson was stunned. "Just when they're needed most. I thought to myself, *How could they do such a thing? Maybe they're having a love affair. With themselves.*"

In a fascinating way, Robertson believes this season amplified his and Muriel's love:

> I made a wonderful discovery. As Muriel became ever more dependent on me, our love seeped to deeper, unknown crevices of the heart.... My imprisonment turned out to be a delightful liberation to love more fully than I had ever known. We found the chains of confining circumstance to be, not instruments of torture, but bonds to hold us closer. But there was even greater liberation. It has to do with God's love. No one ever needed me like Muriel, and no one ever responded to my efforts so totally as she. It's the nearest thing I've experienced on a human plane to what my relationship with God was designed to be: God's unfailing love poured out in constant care of helpless me. Surely he planned that relationship to draw from me the kind of love and gratitude Muriel had for her man. Her insatiable—even desperate—longing to be with me, her quiet confidence in my ability and desire to care for her, a

mirror reflection of what my love for God should be. That was the first discovery—the power of love to liberate in the very bondage imposed by unwanted circumstances. People don't always understand that.

Robertson teaches us that if we want a lifelong love, it is not about how a marriage can fulfill our needs, but how we can fulfill our spouse's needs.

I Do and I Will

It might be the death of infatuation. The birth of kids. The busyness of raising children. The quiet of the empty nest. A sudden change in midlife. Or the medical diagnosis of an aging body. Whatever it is, we can choose to let it be an avenue toward intimacy, drawing us together, or a highway toward gradual separation.

As couples, we can anticipate problems in any one of the above seasons. The default action of the relationship will be to drift away from each other while we attend to the crisis at hand. We have to remember that we made a prior commitment never to leave our spouses behind when we're running toward something else.

Look at your relationship. Talk about it with your spouse. Is he or she suffering because of a power shift? Is your spouse running after you and can't catch you? Is there a power shift I haven't mentioned? How can you grow back together? How can you anticipate and prepare for the next one?

An intimate marriage requires vigilance. Just waking up and going about our days, without giving thought to our marriages, usually leads us to slowly drift apart. As we've already seen, marriage is not like a tree that naturally grows after it's been planted; we must have the mind-set of architects and builders, planning and constructing our marriages stone by stone, brick by brick. Marriage is not like the natural, seemingly accidental beauty of the Grand Canyon; it's far more like the completion of a great cathedral that has slowly taken shape over decades. When couples say "I do" on their wedding days, I wish they'd add "and I will, *every day of our lives*." The catchphrase for an intimate marriage really could be "I do and I will."

Marriage is a bit like snorkeling. We can go underwater for a while, but eventually, we have to come up for air. Life dictates that we may not be able to connect conversationally as often as we would like as a couple; we may have to endure short separations to care for our parents and children; we may not be able to enjoy sex with the frequency we once did. But when the seasons never end, when one season is replaced by another, when a temporary setback becomes a never-ending string of events, our marriages will grow dimmer by the day.

Do you want an increasingly intimate union? Then you must work to stay close. Be eager to get back together when life events force you apart. As a couple, you can hold your breath for only so long. Choose to remind yourselves of those blessed words spoken on your wedding day, "I do," and then add the phrase "and I will."

I do and I will. Try saying that aloud to each other and daily to yourself. That's the road map to a life of shared intimacy and satisfaction.

Building a Lifelong Love

1. Is there a "power imbalance" going on in your marriage right now? Do you feel like you are chasing after your spouse or your spouse is chasing after you? How do you think God would want you to respond to that imbalance at this moment?

2. How can any current challenge in your marriage be turned from pulling the two of you apart to helping you grow together? What's another way to navigate it? Have you talked it out? Are you praying together about it?

3. Do you need to ask forgiveness for any previous irresponsibility during a power imbalance? That is, have you been unkind or perhaps just inattentive when your spouse really needed you to step up but you didn't or you were too engaged elsewhere to notice?

4. If you were to write a "relational prescription" for a couple in precisely your situation of life to keep them growing together instead of apart, what would it be? Write it out. Then start living it.

Heavenly Father, one of the most amazing things about You is that even though You have a universe to run, You never miss a single thing about any one of us. You are an attentive God, astonishingly so, and ever caring, ever involved, ever ready to listen and to love. We want to be like You. In the midst of busy lives, we need You to remind us of what matters most. We need You to help us understand each other, to learn how to read the relational signals that one of us feels alienated or taken for granted. Lord, we want a relationship that pleases You, and we know now that won't happen by accident. We need reminders, we need You to guide our thinking, and we need You to warn us when we start to drift. And so we ask You to do just that. In Jesus's name, amen.

12

Clothed and Ashamed

I slid into the restaurant booth first, and Lisa snuggled up right next to me, giving a little exclamation of delight.

"Oh, are you cold?" asked the young woman sitting across from us.

"No," Lisa said. "He's just been gone all day. I haven't seen him yet."

"Oooooh," the young woman responded.

One of the most healing aspects of marriage for me has been the fact that I live with a woman who knows me better than anyone else ever has or ever will and yet, wonder of wonders, she still likes me. She even respects me. Even with all my particularities, bad habits, and weaknesses, she truly *wants* to be with me.

That brings a lot of healing to a basically insecure man (and says some even more marvelous things about the graciousness of my wife).

Such an acceptance, however, requires one of the things most of us fear: honesty. Yes, power shifts and the seasons of life can tear us apart, but another enemy—dishonesty—constitutes just as big of a threat.

If we want to pursue a true oneness, if we want to keep growing together, we have got to stop with the secrets. Either we are 100 percent married, or we are playacting at marriage. We lose the satisfaction of being fully known and fully loved when we hide from our spouses, because we naturally begin to think, *Sure, she respects me now, but that's only because she doesn't know about x, y, or z.*

Every lie becomes a wedge between the two of you, and here's what's so alarming: the pressures of life will continue to widen that wedge. Lies are never orphans, and they rarely just go away. They have a tendency to multiply and force us to produce legions of other deceits. You start lying, and soon you run out of fingers to count them on. It is impossible to be an intimate mate with your spouse if you are a total stranger to the truth. Intimacy demands authenticity.

Jeremiah 8:5 warns of those who "cling to deceit." All of us do this, in a sense. For me, anyway, whenever there's a tense situation, deceit feels like my natural drift. Someone asks, "Do you really mean what you just said?" I'm surprised by their passion and feebly respond, "Uh, no, of course not." But, really, I did.

Deceit has the potential to push us apart as couples. I'm not suggesting we become brutally frank to the point where we share secrets that serve no purpose other than to hurt our spouses, or that we are obligated to share things that we know will do more harm than good. Counselors have told me that they have heard spouses say things that they know the other spouse will never get over. I'm not talking about sharing things like that. What I am saying, however, is that we live "in the light" with each other. We don't hide who we really are. We don't nurse addictions by covering them up.

My friend, author Juli Slattery, put it this way: "A wife fears rejection from her spouse, so she keeps secrets about struggles, fears, and mistakes. A husband would rather carry his own struggles rather than be vulnerable with his wife. These choices are not loving, but selfishly withholding. However, there are times when love compels us to measure our words. In moments of anger and disappointment, the 'truth' of how you might feel toward your spouse might be crushing and cruel. Sharing intimate details of sexual temptations and failings may deeply wound your spouse. Only by seeking the Lord's wisdom can we discern how to live authentically by sharing boldly while loving deeply."

With that caveat, here's what I've found to be generally true: *If you want to increase the intimacy in your marriage, increase the honesty.*

The First Lie

We can't, of course, be honest with our spouses if we are deceiving ourselves. In their excellent book *Beyond Ordinary*, Justin and Trisha Davis tackle this head-on. Justin had a serious honesty problem at one point in his marriage to Trisha—a problem that grew so severe it resulted in a separation that could have led to divorce.

That experience has led him to regularly ask himself the following questions:

1. Is the fear of the consequences of the truth greater than my commitment to tell the truth?
2. Am I telling myself the truth?
3. Is there a truth I have distorted or am distorting right now?
4. Is there something I have withheld or am currently withholding from my spouse?

You can serve your marital intimacy well by writing down those four questions and regularly going back through them. In the strong fortress of a sacred marriage, we can courageously face the truth about ourselves and each other—because Christ is there to supply the grace, forgiveness, and power to change.

Why not give honesty a try? You're so afraid your spouse won't accept the real you, but how do you know? Yes, there may be moments of real hurt and pain. Yes, you would be wise to work this out with a counselor first if it's going to feel like a major revelation to your spouse.* But do you really prefer holding back and living in fear, never really being known because of what might happen if you

---

* Seriously, if you think there is any chance a disclosure could be particularly painful to your spouse, please talk to a trusted, mature friend or pastor first. This person can then perhaps suggest a counselor if he or she thinks you're correct in your assessment. You must be careful here. One wrong thing, shared in the wrong way and at the wrong time, can become a *lifelong* wound.

start telling the truth? Is that a better choice than taking a risk to become fully known and perhaps, in the face of that, still fully loved?

In our pursuit of a more intimate union, the image of "naked and unashamed" or "covered up and very ashamed" doesn't just refer to whether or not we're wearing clothes. It refers to hiding the very essence of who we truly are. It refers to any lie we might be trying to cover up with "verbal clothes." Being "naked and unashamed" means being able to tell your spouse about the real you, not just showing him or her your physical private parts, but the innermost recesses of your soul. Maybe you need to tell your spouse that you are having trouble at work rather than worry that it might freak him or her out; that your finances may be at risk; maybe it's a minor addiction to alcohol that hasn't become a real problem yet, but it's starting to scare you and you need someone to help you face this new challenge. Such conversations can be terrifying, but they are the doorway to true intimacy.

Duplicity

Young couples often think that a lack of feelings will be the end of their relationship, when in actuality the greater threat is a lack of honesty. A particular type of dishonesty—what we might call duplicity—can do more than just wreck our intimacy and our marriages; it can wreck our souls.

What is this duplicity, and where does it come from?

Duplicity arises whenever we are determined to do something we know is wrong and are equally determined to avoid the consequences of our wrongdoing. Every one of us faces those moments when we know we shouldn't do what we really want to do. The fear of being found out can keep us from making the wrong choice, but duplicity diabolically undercuts this by presenting a twisted solution to our stress: "Here's the way to fulfill your desire: do it, *but lie about it*. You can enjoy the desire *and* avoid the consequences."

Duplicity is simply saying, "A second sin can help you enjoy the first sin," thus *multiplying your sinful desires*.

In opposition, honesty says, "You know this is going to break your spouse's heart. You know the consequences will last much longer than the pleasure. You know you can't maintain an intimate marriage and keep this from your spouse, so why do it?" This helps *crucify your sinful desires*.

Saying a definitive no to sin ultimately leads to less stress. Once the decision is made, the stress is gone. There is nothing to fear when we have done nothing wrong. In telling us to lie, duplicity itself is a lie, as many of us have found out after the consequences of our actions did crash down on our heads and did wound our spouses. While we can choose our actions, we don't always get to choose the consequences. Duplicity lies to us even as it urges us to lie to our spouses.

Duplicity offers short-term satisfaction by murdering, or at least severely maiming, long-term intimacy. It takes us away from ourselves (we can't grow when we become blind to our own hearts), it takes us away from our spouses (you can't maintain authentic intimacy with someone you are lying to), and it takes us away from our God (in the sense of making His voice more distant and making our hearts more callous to His gentle whispers). We have to deaden ourselves (a horrific thought) to the loving voice of the Holy Spirit who is warning us to turn around. More intent on fulfilling the desire than walking in truth, we have to (ouch) train ourselves to shut out God's passionate and loving warnings. This can't be done without severe consequences. Once we start falling from God, we lose touch with how far we have fallen. The less sensitive we are to His voice, the less aware we are of His presence. It is a treacherous place to live. I have seen men and women become mere shells of what they once were after they have cut the tether of sensitivity toward the voice of God and lost a reverence for His commands. It's horrific, in every sense of the word.

If it's true, as I said in *Sacred Marriage*, that God designed marriage in part to make us holy even more than to make us happy, then honesty is one of the key guardrails of that truth. God has given us our spouses as aids to our consciences; when we circumvent our consciences and our accountability to our spouses, it's like breaking *into* prison. God wants to bless us with holiness, but we stupidly jump over the barbed-wire fence and climb into a jail cell, only to be isolated and alone, not fully realizing what we've just done. God wants us to live in the fresh air, in the light, in the beauty of the world He has created. But our desires tell us to flee the light and the fresh air, to climb the fences God has erected for our protection, and to hide ourselves away in isolation, loneliness, and darkness.

Be honest: If you've done something, or are doing something, that you're ashamed of and then lied about, has it ever served you in any true sense? Are you a better person because of it? Do you live with more joy and peace? Are you closer to your spouse and more secure in your spouse's love?

If you are living in duplicity about anything in your marriage—your sexual desires, your eating habits, your spending habits, your recreational habits, your drinking habits—just know that you are paying a high cost. Duplicity never solves the problem of inappropriate desire and fear; it just exacerbates the problem and lets it grow, and the endgame is alienation from all that is holy and true and good.

Why get married only to hide? Why trade "naked and unashamed" for "wearing a costume" and "fearful your mask will fall off"?

Cowardly Duplicity

There's another form of duplicity that we are prone to: we can be less than honest when we need to tell others painful truths. This is the duplicity of a people pleaser. Let's say your husband is acting like a jerk; someone calls him out on it, which offends him even more. Later on, in private, he asks you what you think.

You think he was a jerk, but you say, "He overreacted. You were just being honest."

I've talked to couples where an honest twenty-minute conversation could have spared twenty years of frustration. One woman couldn't bear to tell her husband that he smelled when he came to bed, so she just wasn't that interested in sex. She didn't want to hurt him—who wants to hear their spouse say they smell? But her lack of enthusiasm for sex over the course of two decades hurt him far more than just being honest about his need to take a shower and brush his teeth.

We're going to talk plenty about serving our spouses, loving our spouses, and unconditionally accepting our spouses in the next section, but these challenges shouldn't be understood to mean that we never speak a word of truth to them, if that word of truth would serve them and serve us as a couple.

If you are married to a supremely selfish spouse and never raise the issue, in the end you become an enabler of her selfishness. If you are married to a spouse who presents one image to the church and another image everywhere else, and you go along with it, you are serving his hypocrisy. I'm not talking about *ever* shaming your spouse or calling her out in public (please, for the love of God, *no!*). I'm talking about private conversations in a loving, gentle, and humble manner.

Your spouse may not receive your truth. Once he knows your opinion and won't accept it, it's not duplicity to let it rest for a bit. You're not being duplicitous—you're just being pragmatic. He's not ready to deal with it, and you can't make him. But the key is, you're not pretending, and he knows it, even if you're not nagging him about it.

Do you truly desire marital intimacy—that blessed sense of being one? Then you must rid yourself of all duplicity in your life and marriage. Resolve today that you'll let holy fear (God's loving warning) overcome your desires rather than lead you to a place of compromise that is in actuality a place of ruin. Let your pursuit of a more intimate union motivate you to share some hard truths rather than exist in an artificial intimacy sustained by fearful lies.

Be forewarned: the weight of the lies we tell each other increases through the years. After thirty years of marriage, when Lisa slid next to me in that restaurant booth and snuggled up to me just because she hadn't seen me all day, it made me feel like a king. If I had been lying to her, it would have made me feel like an impostor. I would have felt threatened, not comforted, and ashamed, not loved. And the longer it had been going on, the more frightening it would have been. Her expression of intimacy would have been painful, as I would have thought, *If only she knew ...*

But she does know, and so we enjoy the blessed fruit of being naked and unashamed. There are millionaires who would trade all their money and success for a middle-class life if only they could be "naked and unashamed" again—especially with their spouses. They know that success while living in the dark isn't *truly* living. The only way to be truly happy and successful lies in being able to be "naked and unashamed"—in front of our parents, our kids, God, and most definitely our spouses.

Building a Lifelong Love

1. This is a tough question right off the top, but I'm going to ask it: What is your worst deceit in marriage, as you read this? What should your spouse know that he or she doesn't know? Who can

you talk to in order to consider whether this is something you
need to share? *counseling in earlier years*

2. I mentioned that I've talked to couples where "an honest
   twenty-minute conversation could have spared twenty years of
   frustration." Is there an issue in your marriage that is ongoing
   that you've been afraid to bring up? In other words, question
   1 asked if there was a personal deception. This question asks if
   there is a relational deception. Prayerfully consider how (and
   whether) you should bring this up with your spouse.

3. What are two or three ways that you can make your spouse feel
   more secure in your love so that he or she will feel more confident
   in being honest with you? Does your spouse have any reason
   to feel insecure? Are you doing something or regularly saying
   something that might make your spouse feel legitimately fearful
   to "walk in the light"?

*Our Holy Father, Your Son described Himself as "the truth" and said
He spoke only what is true. Redeemed by Him, we want to live in the
light as He is in the light. Wash us with Your acceptance, for we know
that You are for us even in our sins. Convince us of how You have completely forgiven us, so that we will have the confidence of being dearly
loved children. Resensitize us to the gentle but firm conviction of Your
Holy Spirit. Let us hate duplicity more than we hate self-denial. Give
us hearts that want to walk in purity. Give us a new vision of the joy
of being fully known and fully accepted and fully loved by each other,
and give us the courage to pursue it. In Jesus's name, amen.*

13

The Two Dimensions
of Marriage

"Can you help us resolve a disagreement?"

The young couple looked at Lisa and me so eagerly we couldn't deny them.

"Well, we can try."

"We're about to get our first tax refund check, and we're trying to decide how to divide it up."

"What do you mean, divide it up?" Lisa asked.

"Well, should the person who earned 60 percent of the income get 60 percent of the refund, or should we just split it down the middle?"

This couple had far more fundamental issues than how to divide up a tax refund; they were existing as two distinct individuals, and that goes against God's purpose for marriage.

Pursuing a more intimate union means wrestling with how radical this notion is that two people become one. This pursuit, though glorious, will go against every selfish fiber in our being. Many people want intimacy in the abstract more than they want it in reality—we want the benefits of being known and loved, but we hate the process of dying to ourselves that it takes to get there. We're a little like the people who want to become famous but then, once they become famous and have to live with the hassles, wish they could become anonymous again. Some of us get married thinking we really want a life of intimacy, but once the challenges and burdens of intimacy press in on us, we want to go back to being selfish and estranged.

Here's what you need to know: Once you get married, everything changes. Everything. Even something like sin becomes a shared burden. Nothing is faced alone. There is no dividing up, because you can't divide one person without killing him, and you can't divide spouses without killing the marriage.

It's a spiritual law: the more you "divide up" as a couple, the farther apart you grow. If you want to become one, you've got to think of yourself as one, perhaps in a deeper way than you ever have before.

I love the way early church father John Chrysostom put this: "You no longer have a body of your own (since you gave it away in marriage), yet you have money of your own? After marriage, you are no longer two, but one flesh, and are your possessions still divided? Love of money! You have both become one person, one organism, and can you still say, 'my own'?"[1] Chrysostom wrote this sixteen hundred years ago, and couples are still struggling with it today! Questions about "mine" and "yours" may be relevant to couples sorting through a divorce but never to couples who are pursuing marital intimacy. The very notion of "mine" and "yours" means you are living separate lives.

When the Bible says the "two shall become one," it's referring to a true spiritual joining of souls. To enjoy the full benefits of marriage, we have to start thinking like one, tackling every problem as one, taking care of each other as one. If a husband notices that a wife is getting too tired, working too hard, not taking care of herself, that becomes *his* problem, even if perhaps he would, individually, benefit from her continuing to work that hard. If a wife senses that her husband is discouraged, that discouragement becomes *her* discouragement and she had best find ways to build her husband up rather than derive any sick satisfaction from momentarily achieving the "stronger" hand.

Becoming one means I care as much about her problems as mine; that I cherish her health, her well-being, her pleasure as much as I cherish mine. If she becomes ill, I don't feel sorry for myself, as if I'm not ill and have to care for her. My attitude should be, "This is what we need to do to get better." My wife is not a servant to be used; she is part of me and I am part of her. If I poison *my* mind with lust, I'm poisoning *our* marital bed. If I get reckless with *my* wallet, I'm putting *our* account at risk. I can't do anything that won't affect her, so I want to not only watch out for her but to actively seek out and serve her well-being. I would never put on one shoe and walk out in the snow, feeling smug that one foot is covered and warm. That would be foolish and borderline mentally disturbed. Yet many "couples" live that way; as long as they, as individuals, get their way, they are astonishingly unconcerned about their other "foot."

You see, under Jesus's teaching, divorce isn't an amputation—it's a death, the death of a united soul.

There can be no marital intimacy if two individuals refuse to die as individuals and be reborn as a couple.

Let me be explicit here: if you've never done this—intentionally died as an individual to be reborn as one-half of a couple—if you've never chosen to work at growing as one, you don't know what marriage to each other would truly be like. You're roommates, perhaps, maybe even best friends, but you're not *married* in the fullest sense of the word. If you're disappointed in a disconnected marriage to your current spouse, that doesn't mean you'd be disappointed in a connected and intimate marriage to your current spouse. Instead of changing spouses, why not first try changing "disconnected" to "connected" and see how it goes?* You've discovered that you loathe living together as mere roommates, but why not give intimate marriage a try?

The Bigger Picture

Pursuing oneness isn't just about becoming closer as husband and wife—it's about sharing in a blessed and sacred reality that Jesus said mirrors the Trinity itself. In the gospel of John, Jesus prayed

---

* Some of you might be screaming, "But my spouse doesn't want to be this connected to me!" We'll deal with this situation in the next chapter.

to His heavenly Father, "[I ask] that they may all be one, even as You, Father, are in Me and I in You, that they also may be in Us, so that the world may believe that You sent Me. The glory which You have given Me I have given to them, that they may be one, just as We are one; I in them and You in Me, that they may be perfected in unity, so that the world may know that You sent Me, and loved them, even as You have loved me" (John 17:21–23 NASB).

God is clearly into "oneness."

Marriage is a "minichurch," a microscopic cell out of which God can begin to build an intimate community. By living faithfully with our spouses, we can learn the skills, mind-set, and spiritual principles necessary to understand how this vision of Jesus is to be fleshed out in a wider community. Jesus seems to suggest that becoming one with another person helps us to experience God in His fullness. Most churches are focused on becoming *larger*, which is understandable given the Great Commission. But we are also called to become *closer*—in a very real spiritual sense, to become one.

I don't know how to become one as a group. I don't have a clue. (My good friend Dr. Mike Dittman *is* an expert at this and is doing some marvelous work with churches. See www.havenfortheheart .com.) But I can begin with my own marriage.

Here's the thing: If we can't keep our marriages together, we won't keep our churches together. If we can't keep our churches together, we won't do a very good job of proclaiming the unity of the Godhead to the world. If I can figure out how to increasingly become one with my wife, along the way I'm going to develop skills to become one with a pastoral staff, with coworkers, with church members. These other relationships won't even begin to approach the intimacy of marriage, of course, even as the intimacy of marriage won't even begin to approach the intimacy within the Trinity. But it can still be a glorious glimpse nonetheless.

Some of you are no doubt asking, "But *how*, Gary, *how* do we become one?" If you look back at the chapters in this section, you'll see we've already laid the groundwork: we have to be intentional during the different seasons of marriage; we have to choose to build authentic intimacy instead of artificial intimacy; we have to be absolutely honest with each other.

Now we're going to look at three other tools in this chapter. The first is learning to ask the right question.

The Tale of Two Questions

Becoming one requires a fundamental shift in our thinking. Every aspect of marriage has to be looked at through an "Abrahamic" lens. Back in the time of Abraham, before Israel even existed, God chose an individual and made an amazing promise: "I will bless you … so that you will be a blessing" (Gen. 12:2 NRSV).

In the New Testament, Peter saw being a blessing as a basic Christian practice: "Do not repay evil for evil or abuse for abuse; but, on the contrary, repay with a blessing. It is for this that you were called—that you might inherit a blessing" (1 Pet. 3:9 NRSV). Notice blessing is urged in the midst of conflict, not just in happy, peaceful harmony. Because God has blessed me, I am called to be a blessing to others. He has taken care of my greatest needs, so now I can focus on taking care of yours.

Thus, there are two questions we can ask within marriage that will take us to two entirely different dimensions—intimacy or estrangement. We have to choose which dimension we want to live in. We can ask:

"How can I bless you?"

Or:

"How can I get my needs met?"

If we live in the second dimension ("How can I get my needs met?"), every conflict will be resolved in terms of how we benefit from the outcome, even at our spouses' expense. That's thinking like an individual. If we live in the first dimension ("How can I bless you?"), every conflict will be resolved in terms of how our spouses are blessed in the process. That's thinking like we're one, and it leads to greater intimacy.

This is spiritual *and* cognitive. I've got to pray to God that He will change my heart so that I truly desire to bless my spouse, even if I'm disappointed in her, frustrated with her, or angry with her. And cognitively, I have to choose to look at every moment of marriage as a way to purposefully bless my wife.

Most marital disagreements result from living in the second dimension: "What causes fights and quarrels among you? … You covet but you cannot get what you want" (James 4:1–2). Instead of quarreling, I should ask myself, "What's the best way to bless my spouse in this situation?"

Does living in the first dimension mean we become "sacred door-mats"? Absolutely not. It all depends on the content of the word *bless*.

For instance, in a real-life scenario, a wife told me that her husband said, "Quit throwing away my pornography. I need it. If you throw away my pornography, I'm throwing away your Bible."

Her desire is that her husband not keep a stash of pornography. That's what she wants. But it's also what will most bless her husband. So she doesn't give way and allow him to maintain a separate sexual life apart from their intimacy. She blesses him by saying, "No, I won't stand for this." Sometimes what we want can also be a blessing to our spouses, even if they don't want it. To bless other people is to seek their ultimate good, and their ultimate good is what draws them to God.

A husband might bless his wife by truly wanting her to consider a healthier style of life. He might want her to be released to enjoy sexual intimacy more freely and more often. Of course, he would benefit from both these aims, but if he is driven by a desire to bless her, not to get what he wants, he will still be living in the first dimension.

Living in the first dimension is all about cultivating hearts that are inspired and empowered by the Holy Spirit—being blessed by God and living to pass that blessing down to others. This is the only sustaining basis for a truly sacred marriage.

Our spouses can usually tell if we are pursuing the first or second dimension. I can't explain why, but there's just a different tone, a different attitude that comes out of us when we live by the first dimension than when we selfishly pursue the second.

If you skip over the spiritual (or heart) aspect and seek to "change" your spouse for your own good out of selfish intentions, you can do great harm, even when you're in the right. It's possible to be right in the wrong way and for the wrong reasons. When we are fighting for the right out of selfish concerns, that's still a miserable place to live because then it's all about "conquering your spouse" or "winning the argument," not growing in understanding, empathy, and love. A victorious general might feel adrenaline and elation when he defeats an army, but he definitely doesn't feel close or intimate with them.

Every time you enter a conflict, every morning when you feel that selfish heart start to chirp, every evening when you look back over the day and start to feel resentment, attack it with the first dimension. Ask yourself, "How can I bless my spouse, right here, right now?"

Sometimes, blessing our spouses requires us to "kill" something about ourselves. This is yet another tool to build marital oneness.

Killing Spiders

When the spider dropped in front of me, I killed it.

Part of me hates doing this. Spiders don't hurt anyone. In fact, they serve a good purpose—they kill other insects. Personally, I have nothing against spiders.

But they can make webs. And they bother Lisa. She hates them. So I kill them.

Because I'm married to Lisa, I've made a prior commitment that her feelings outweigh mine on a lot of matters, and the killing of spiders is one of them. I don't rethink this every time I see a new spider; because I'm married to Lisa, it's already decided: if I see a spider in the house, I kill it so she doesn't have to. If it's right near an outside door, she's happy to let me push it over the threshold; but if it's in an inner room, that spider is history.

If Lisa's dad had been an alcoholic (he certainly wasn't), I'd kill all alcohol use in my life. I don't have a theological problem with alcohol, but that wouldn't matter; out of love for Lisa, if she were sensitive toward the potential devastation of alcohol abuse, I wouldn't want her to worry. I'd just kill alcohol use and avoid it altogether.

If Lisa and I were on our second marriages and Lisa's first marriage had been destroyed by excessive video game playing, I'd kill that too. I'd just think, *She's going to be especially sensitive to that. Every time I pick up a controller, it's going to resurrect a lot of bad feelings from her past. Rather than ask her to reset those deep-seated anxieties, I think it's best if I just kill that part of my life.*

Some of you might be thinking, *Hey, that's not fair! I like alcohol and video games—why should I give them up just because my spouse has a problem with them?*

My friends, that was a discussion to have *before* you got married. When I'm working with premarital couples, I'm searching for any spiders I can find to help the couple understand each other so they can make an informed choice. I'll ask them, "Is an intimate union with this person worth more than this temporary diversion?" Once you're already married, however, you've sort of made the choice by default—if, that is, you truly want to become one.

The pursuit of marital intimacy requires agreeing to kill certain spiders that bug our spouses, *just because they bug our spouses*. Scripture may not prohibit these spiders. They may not be inherently wrong. But if they cause our spouses pain, that's good enough reason to kill them. It's all part of becoming one.

Do you see how this blessing mentality, living in the first dimension of marriage, changes everything? It's not about my rights; it's about what will bless my spouse.

Two people can't become one without a little sanding taking place. If you're going to glue two things together, you sand them to make sure they fit. Edges need to be rubbed off. The same thing is true in marriage. If I want to become one with Lisa, parts of me have to die. If I refuse to let them die, I'm refusing to become one. Instead of saying, "I do," I'm saying, "I won't."

What are you letting live that is killing your marital intimacy? Do you know what your spouse's spiders are? If you value intimacy, if you value truly becoming one, do the loving thing: hunt those spiders down and kill them.

I Was Born for This!

One of the things that inhibits the growth of marital intimacy is when we start to focus on the difficulties of loving our spouses rather than focusing on how we can bless them. The truth is, we get married for mostly selfish reasons, so when we're not getting what we want anymore, we can resent rather than appreciate our marriages. But if we live in the first dimension of marriage, with a true blessing mentality, when troubles arise, we'll adopt the attitude of Proverbs 17:17: "A friend loves at all times, and a brother is born for a time of adversity."

A good fireman doesn't resent getting a call in the middle of the night; that's what he has been trained to do—put out fires. In the same way, if we believe we are "born" to bear our spouses' adversities, we'll be eager to rise to the challenge instead of resenting the intrusion. We become "firemen" to our spouses, eager to help at any moment.

Imagine wives with husbands suffering long bouts of unemployment or addiction rising up to say, "I was *born* for this! I can love my man in the midst of this!" Remember, we approach each issue as a couple. If my left arm is broken, my right arm doesn't complain that it has to do all the work. My body is a unit, and when any part is lacking, another part steps up. That's the goal of a truly intimate marriage.

Imagine husbands married to women who are gravely ill, or sexually wounded and suffering the psychological consequences, or struggling with their roles as moms, or frustrated in their careers in a way that leaves them with nasty attitudes, and their husbands take up this biblical challenge and proclaim, "I can do this! I can love this woman! I was *born* to do this!"

Instead of seeing a weakness or limitation as a point of frustration, we are called to let adversity call out and even showcase our commitment. A biblical friend doesn't love only in wealth, health, social success, and on sunny days. A biblical friend loves at all times. So, instead of feeling sorry for ourselves when our spouses hit a dry spell, or when they are going through a difficult time, let's lace up our shoes a little tighter and remind ourselves, "Here we go: I was born for this, to love this person at all times, even in adversity."

I Am Yours

Let's quickly review the journey to become one before we wrap up this chapter:

- We have to thoughtfully navigate the different seasons of marriage so that we are sharing in life, not just acting as teammates.
- We have to choose to build authentic intimacy instead of artificial intimacy.
- We have to be honest with each other.
- We have to adopt a blessing mentality, asking, "How can I bless my spouse?" instead of, "How can I get my needs met?"
- We kill the "spiders" in our lives that annoy our spouses.
- We view our spouses' weaknesses and limitations as pathways to shared intimacy by adopting the attitude of "I was born for this!"

These are all part of the journey toward oneness. The more you become one as a couple, the happier and more satisfied you will be in your marriage. None of this happens by accident. Two people can find themselves falling in love, but nobody "falls" into intimate oneness. That's a deliberate choice and a long journey.

Here's the endgame: my prayer is that the day would come when the two of you can say to each other in the fullest sense of the words, "I am yours."

When you get back together after a long day at work, and your wife puts her car keys down, sighs, and says, "What a day," can you make the mental adjustment to care and say, "Tell me all about it"? If you learn to do this, what you're really telling her is "I am yours. I belong to you. Right now, this moment, you matter more to me than anyone or anything else."

It may be even more difficult to stay engaged, men, if your wife catches *you* saying "What a day" and asks you about it. Our male minds tend to think, *The last thing I want to do is relive that day by recounting it*, but our wives want to know. By our answer, they want to hear us say, "I am yours." Men, how awesome would it be to knowingly come home to a wife who already knew the problems you were going to face that day at work because you told her about them the night before? Now she can celebrate with you, commiserate with you, encourage you, or back you up. Regardless of how the situation turned out, it helped draw the two of you together into a more intimate union. You may not have succeeded at work, but you won the battle at home, and home is where you live; work is only where you visit.

When either partner has sexual desires (not even needs, desires are enough), will each partner say to the other, "I am yours"?

When an extended family member has a crisis at a really inconvenient time—a work deadline, a scheduled trip to go hunting or run a marathon—will we hold our plans loosely and say to our concerned spouse, "I am yours"? Or will our actions say, "I am yours—after I am my boss's, or my hobby's, or anything else's ..."

If your wife has a party she really wants to attend but you have a game you really want to watch, if your husband has a hobby you really don't enjoy but you see the pleasure it gives him when you're there supporting him, if your spouse has a season when he or she needs extra care, will you *still* say, "I am yours"?

On the day you got married, a roomful of people and your God heard you tell your spouse, "I am yours."

So, are you?

Today?

In every way?

Building a Lifelong Love

1. Does the notion of oneness, a very high level of intimacy, frighten you or make you even more eager to experience it? What do you think you need to do to welcome the thought of true marital intimacy in your life? What are your fears and concerns?

2. Consider your last marital disagreement. Was your attitude "How can I get my needs met?" or "How can I bless you?" Do

you think it's realistic that the latter can become your default position?

3. Take a moment to think about some "spiders" you need to kill in order to become more intimately connected with your spouse. Remember, spiders don't have to be morally wrong—they might just be about your spouse's preferences. Is there a spider you can kill that will help the two of you become closer? Is the alternative worth hanging on to?

4. If a friend is "born for adversity," just like a firefighter is born to fight fires, what specifically, as this applies to your marriage, were you born for?

5. If you honestly evaluated your heart and your actions (looking at them separately, just for the sake of discussion), where would you rate your response in regard to your marriage?

In my heart:

1 —— 2 —— 3 —— 4 —— 5 —— 6 —— 7 —— 8 —— 9 —— 10

I am mostly mine   I am yours

In my actions:

1 —— 2 —— 3 —— 4 —— 5 —— 6 —— 7 —— 8 —— 9 —— 10

I am mostly mine   I am yours

6. Based on the results of question 5, are you where you want to be? If not, what do you need to change in order to get there?

Our creator God, You designed marriage to make two people one. Your Son, Jesus, said that the reason most divorces should be unthinkable is because You have made the two one. Help us to be what You have already declared us to be. Give us the grace, day by day, to ask You how we can bless each other instead of how our needs can be met. Show us what we need to do to root out of our lives anything that is blocking a growing sense of oneness. Let us become especially one rather than estranged when we face life's trials and each other's limitations. Let us begin to experience the oneness You share with Your Son, that we might testify through our marriage to the truth that You are who You are. In Jesus's name, amen.

14

Loving Someone Who Doesn't Care

All this talk about oneness might be painful for some of you, as you might be married to a spouse who doesn't want to become one. What does it mean to be faithfully married to someone who honestly just doesn't care about pursuing a more intimate union?

Jason faced this in his marriage to Maria. He finally had to accept that he and Maria wanted something entirely different out of the same marriage. They've been together for fifteen years, and it has taken Jason that long to realize that his and his wife's visions of a successful marriage are worlds apart.

Jason's situation is the opposite of what most speakers and writers like me usually talk about; we typically say it's the wife who seems more relational, but in this case, Jason is the one who desires the soulful discussions and a commitment to work on the relationship. Maria says she wants that too, in the abstract, but the only talk she initiates is about surface things: decorating the house, what the kids need done, or something her mother told her. She never asks Jason how he's doing, what he's feeling, or how he thinks the relationship is going—even though he has repeatedly expressed his desire that she do that.

It doesn't take a PhD in therapy to know that Jason needs and desires a certain level of intimacy that Maria doesn't. Maria is willing to live on the surface. As long as she and Jason do "fun" things (according to Maria's definition) and take care of the house and family, she's happy in her marriage. The fact that Jason isn't happy with that doesn't seem to bother her—at least, not enough to make her do anything about it.

I asked Jason, "How do you go deeper with someone who doesn't want to go deeper? Help me help other readers."

It's not an easy question. "Fixing" a relationship isn't like fixing a car—one intelligent being acting on an inanimate thing. A relationship between two individuals requires cooperation. Ideally, Jason's desire to go deeper, his request that Maria occasionally initiate relationship-based discussions, would be enough to motivate her. Those are legitimate desires that most wives would welcome. But apparently Jason's pain isn't her pain and isn't motivation for Maria to change.

What I admire about Jason, however, is that, while recognizing all this, he is still engaged in the marriage. He's not checking out. He realizes that God doesn't call us to love only unselfish spouses. In fact, Jesus specifically said that He excels in loving the "ungrateful and wicked" (Luke 6:32–35) and told us to love just as He loves (v. 36). Later in that same passage, Jesus added, "Give, and it will be given to you" (v. 38), but He didn't say the person doing the giving back will be your spouse. If we love out of reverence for God, we will receive God's comfort. Giving to get is the world's view of love, but it's not Christ's.

Those are my theoretical words, but here is Jason's real-life response. I asked Jason, as one who has struggled with this for more than a decade, "What do you do when you realize that your spouse isn't going to meet legitimate desires?" Jason said:

- "Get the needs met secondarily, through appropriate channels." For Jason, this means building rich relationships with others, though not with women on their own. It's not ideal, but it helps. Jason has some solid friendships with guys, and he and Maria have some healthy couple relationships. Though Jason wouldn't meet any of the wives on their own, he finds that sometimes he can initiate couple-related conversations with another couple that Maria might engage in.

- "Remember, someone has it worse." Jason has a close friend whose wife left him after twelve years of marriage. This guy, according to Jason, is "as solid as they come." Among the many things his friend has had to adjust to is that, due to the separation and subsequent divorce, it's been two years since he's had sex. "I can't say I'm happy with where Maria and I are at sexually," Jason admits. "At most, we have sex once a week.

But I can't even imagine going two years, so I try to be thankful for what I have rather than focus too much on what I don't." Some of you wives may be married to men who don't pray with your kids or talk about Scripture, but they do provide, they do teach your kids about playing sports, they do take your family to church. You don't have *everything* you want, but can you be thankful for what you *do* have, that you wouldn't have if you were on your own?

- "Choose to dwell on the positive, however limited and imperfect it may be." Jason lives by Philippians 4:8: "Finally, brethren, whatever is true, whatever is honorable, whatever is right, whatever is pure, whatever is lovely, whatever is of good repute, if there is any excellence and if anything worthy of praise, *dwell on these things*" (NASB). Jason emphasizes the last phrase, "*dwell on these* things." "You don't want to consistently talk or even pray your marriage down. Focus on the strengths, build on the strengths, and thank God for what you *do* have."

Now I want you to meet Melissa, who has had to face a somewhat similar situation from a different perspective. Her story can add to our understanding of how to be married to someone who doesn't seem to care.

But You Have God

Blessed are the people whose God is the LORD!
—Psalm 144:15 NASB

Melissa is married to a depressed husband. Depression is a tremendous challenge to any marriage. This is not to make people who suffer from depression feel worse about themselves (Charles Spurgeon, the "Prince of Preachers," wrote about suffering various bouts of depression in his book *Lectures to My Students*); it is simply a plea to be honest about the difficult road some married believers tread. Depressed people tend to cast a pall not only on their own lives but also on those around them. Sadly, they often become their own worst enemies, fighting their brain chemistry's resolve to drag them down on a daily basis. Again, I'm not slamming depressed people when I say this; no one chooses to become depressed, and many who do become depressed fight their brain chemistry with valiant effort. I hurt for them; I don't judge them. Unfortunately, valiant effort doesn't always work, and drugs don't always kick in. I'm just trying to be honest here. When you're married to a spouse who doesn't really care about anything, that will mean, in the end, they also don't care as much about the marriage as you do. Even though you know it's not their fault, it's still a difficult road to travel because it can go on for decades.

Quite understandably, there are times when Melissa has had enough. She gets tired of dealing with her husband's depression. But she told me something that is filled with faith. After describing what she deals with on a daily basis, she added, "But I have God, and having God, even if everything else in my life goes wrong—literally, everything else—I am still blessed beyond measure, blessed beyond what I deserve."

Her life verse is Psalm 144:15: "Blessed are the people whose God is the LORD!" (NASB).

That's real faith. That's the courage of a woman of God who recognizes that there are things in this life—including in marriage—that God chooses not to fix, or we resist His fix, and they remain ongoing struggles for the rest of our lives. But will we truly find refuge in the biblical truth that, even if we are disappointed in our marriages, pushed beyond human endurance, "blessed are the people whose God is the LORD"?

God may not heal your marriage. He may not change or heal your spouse. But isn't it true that if we are in Christ, even if nothing else in our lives goes right, we are supremely blessed to have God's fellowship and the promise of a joy-filled eternity?

Whenever I find myself complaining—about anything—I now try to remind myself, "But I have God," and then repeat, "Blessed are the people whose God is the LORD!"

A Sacred Sabbath

To some of you, what we've said up to this point might sound a little idealistic. Let's get practical. The heart is a muscle as much as it is the center of emotion, and muscles need to rest and recover. Sports physiologists explain how rest is a crucial part of conditioning; without it, our muscles will break down.

Relationships are no different.

If you're married to an unusually selfish person, a controlling person, a depressed person, or even if you're wed to just an average sinner, on some days you may say to yourself, "Today, I just need a short break."

That's okay. The idea of a Sabbath was God's, after all. Even when you're married to an agreeable person, at various times the two of you will butt heads, and you'll need to occasionally take a break so that you can look at the situation with fresh eyes and renewed energy.

You're not taking a break from your marriage, of course, but you are trying to take a break from "fixing" your marriage or even working on your marriage. You need to catch your breath, sink your spiritual roots a little deeper, for the next season. Take whatever good is offered, and just let everything else go. One thing I've noticed: people who are always trying to make their marriages "better" rarely feel satisfied. They focus so much on what is wrong that they can never enjoy what's right. If you examine any marriage under a microscope, you'll find plenty to be frustrated about. No, your marriage isn't perfect—it might be far from it—but can't you now and then take a breather from trying to fix it and thank God you've got someone who is still by your side?

There's a big difference between escape and refreshment. A biblical Sabbath of refreshment points back to work; indeed, the very command of the Sabbath is also a command to work: "*Six days you shall labor and do all your work*, but the seventh day is a sabbath to the LORD your God. On it you shall not do any work" (Exod. 20:9–10).

We rest so that we can become even more engaged in the future, asking God to refresh us in order that we might fulfill His high call to "work"—including the work of loving our spouses and children. It's like sharpening the saw: we're doing something besides the direct work we're called to because in the end it will help us complete that work at a higher level.

If you're experiencing a difficult time in your marriage, one of the best things you can do is to get out and laugh—find a few friends, rent a comedy, read a long novel, go on a retreat.* We are limited human beings with finite resources, yet the Bible calls us to a supernatural love beyond our strength. That should teach us two things: we need to radically depend on the Holy Spirit's empowerment, and we need to occasionally take breaks.

Good for you for being so conscientious toward your family responsibilities! But remember—you're running a marathon. You can't keep sprinting. Sometimes, you need to rest.

Before we leave this topic, I want to address those of you who are less engaged in your marriage than your spouse is. You may not think of yourself as selfish (like Maria) or depressed (like Melissa's husband), but you have to admit, you've taken your spouse for granted, and you just don't possess much desire to go deeper in your marriage. Will you listen to one final plea? I think you'll find a big payoff if you consider it.

---

* If enjoying yourself is difficult for you or makes you feel guilty, please consider my book *Pure Pleasure: Why Do Christians Feel So Bad About Feeling Good?* (Grand Rapids, MI: Zondervan, 2009).

Be Kind to Your Spouse's Vulnerability

Craig had been disengaged in his marriage for years. Work came before everything. His wife, Grace, had challenged him about his schedule and obsessive focus many times, but he always chose work over her. Grace fought bitterness every day of her life.

Something happened—too long to tell here—that finally broke Craig's spirit. He understood that the cost of continuing to succeed at the level he had achieved would mean continuing to fail in his marriage to a really good woman. Then one evening that Grace will never forget, Craig sat across from her in a restaurant, grabbed her hand, looked her in the eye, and finally said, "I'm so sorry. We're making a major change. I'm willing to move. I'm going to accept that position we talked about, in a new town, a slower town, a town where you and I can reconnect. *We can be happy again.*"

Grace's tears provided her only needed response. She was thinking, *Anywhere but here. Any job but the one that has pulled us apart.*

Grace had felt trapped—and, in a way, she was. When you are married to someone who isn't acting married toward you, you feel stuck. They have you. They can use that power to bless you or to make you miserable.

Husbands feel vulnerable too, in their own ways. If a wife won't relax but continues to verbally cut her husband up every moment he's home, if she treats the bedroom like a leper's colony to be avoided at all costs, if she puts more energy into the family she supposedly left (her siblings and parents) than the one she's supposed to be building, her husband is left hanging.

It's sobering to realize, in a spirit of kindness and compassion, just how vulnerable our spouses are to us. We can make them miserable. We can all but push them toward despair. Not just in what we do but often in what we don't do—the malice of withholding.

Let's be sensitive toward this vulnerability. Let's be kind in this situation. It is an awesome power, a frightening responsibility. When I saw Grace's tears as she recounted what Craig had said, it made me melt toward Lisa all over again—I want to do that for her. To find something that has been frustrating her, some place in our life or marriage where she has felt trapped, and release her and watch the happiness flood her soul.

On the day we got married, we gained a powerful monopoly—we started to become our spouses' best friends, exclusive lovers, most immediate spiritual supports, and financial partners. The only love life any of our spouses can enjoy is the love life we choose to give to them; do we treat this as a challenge to rise to our best, to be thoughtful, generous, and enthusiastic lovers, or do we shame them for needing us and relying on us?

Are we truly engaged in our marriages? Are we making an honest effort to become one? Or are we coasting, letting the days pass without expressing our love and devotion?

The only spiritual union within marriage your spouse will ever know is the spiritual union you share with him or her; are you going to allow your fears, insecurities, or lack of interest in prayer and shared fellowship become a dead end in your marriage?

Your spouse has only one spouse to connect with, talk to, and relate to emotionally. If you shut him or her down, there are no other spouses waiting to pick up the slack. (There may be plenty of would-be lovers waiting in the wings, but let's not go there.)

How might your spouse be feeling vulnerable today? Will you pray about it? Will you even listen to see if God brings anything to mind? Will you seek to set your spouse free from this trap? Even if you've been denied so much, is there anything your spouse is being denied?

Let's be kind toward our spouses' vulnerabilities.

For those of you who are tearing up as you read this, stinging with the realization of how callous your spouse has been in the face of your vulnerability, let me offer a little scriptural encouragement before we close.

A Double Dose of Good

Confession: Lisa and I have one of the worst backyards in our neighborhood. You are free to feel sorry for my wife. A couple of times a week, I think, *Gary, you really need to do something here*, but I never feel motivated enough to actually do anything.

If there is any defense, I struggle to find a day off every ten or twelve days. I shoot for one day off every seven, but many times, working two jobs (what I've been doing for eighteen years as a writer and speaker and now on the teaching team at Second Baptist, Houston), it's not always possible to find a full nontravel day to get refreshed. So I'm often tired and can think of a dozen other things that need to be done.

Second, I just don't enjoy that kind of thing. Some men live for their yards, with an arsenal of tools and fertilizers and sprays that would make a professional gardener proud. Me? I prefer to be surrounded by books rather than chemicals.

Without the will and the work, you get a backyard that looks like … ours.

There's another place where the absence of will and work wreaks havoc, and that's in marriage. Some of you may be in a relationship that your spouse values about as much as I value our backyard. If your marriage would just "happen," they'd enjoy it. If they already had it, they'd be willing to delight in it. But they lack the will and the work ethic to make the relationship grow. There are other priorities that drive them. Perhaps *you're* the one who is not making your marriage a priority.

Philippians 2:13 is an encouraging word in both instances, as it points us to that all-important double dose of good. "It is God who is at work in you, enabling you both to will and to work for his good pleasure" (NRSV).

The two things we really need in order to build a successful long-term marriage, the will and the work, are the two things that Paul promised God would provide (and there's actually a third element we'll get to in just a moment).

Marriage changes when we stop doing it alone. When we stop trying to make ourselves feel something, when we stop trying to muster up some kind of hope and instead go to the one sure hope we have and pray, "God, please give me the will to make this marriage work, for Your good pleasure."

Do you think God will hesitate before answering that prayer? Do you think He might pause and say, "Hmm, not sure I'm ready to offer that"?

Not a chance. When we lack the will to build a marriage that gives God pleasure, He will be our most enthusiastic advocate. If you feel one-sided in your marriage, it's easy to lose the will. If you've been unsuccessful in bringing about change, it's natural to lose the will. If you've tried every trick you can think of and your bookshelf is filled with every book on marriage published in the last ten years and yet your marriage is still subpar, it's natural just to give up.

Have you prayed for God to give you the will? Do you keep praying, living in an attitude of spiritual dependence, or are you trying to make yourself care? "God, I'm tired of trying to care. I need Your motivation. I need Your will because mine is gone."

And then we're told God also enables us to work. We all know there is plenty of work involved in building and maintaining a marriage, and it's human nature that when there is work involved, we can think of a dozen other things to do. I could clip that bush that is growing out our back fence, *or* I could go for a run. I could take care of that outdoor cabinet with a door that has fallen off its hinge, *or* I could catch up on that news show.

Paul promises us that God will work within us, if we go to Him, if we revere Him (Phil. 2:12). God enables us to work, a powerful divine force and energy lifting us above our apathy and limitations. God becomes the third partner, the uniting presence.

The third element I hinted at is the joy: God offers up the will and the work "for his good pleasure." God will give us the will and the work because doing so pleases Him. He loves to see us live in unity. He delights in seeing us raise godly children in a God-honoring home. He rejoices when a marriage testifies to the relationship between Christ and the church. He finds great satisfaction in seeing two of His children share loyalty and love. Do you think God is content to have His children grow up in a home where Christ is a stranger, love is something the couple used to feel, and joy is a reality that visits on rare occasions? God wants you to have an intimate marriage even more than you do.

I know prayer seems curious at times; we are tempted to ask, "God, if You want this so much, why not just give it without us having to ask?" But that's the way He works. He's a relational God, and He wants us to depend on Him on an ongoing basis. It's the whole manna thing, one day at a time. Sacred marriage isn't about shopping once a month at Costco (i.e., going to God every now and then to get restocked) but rather going to the farmer's market on a daily basis to get our vegetables. It needs to become a daily (and for some of you, hourly) experience. Don't ask me why—I'm not the one who set up this world. It's just the way God wishes it. If you are in a solitary marriage, you have to get this down—learn to shop *every day* at the farmer's market of God's provision.

So let's tap into this divine resource. We're not alone in our marriages, even in our so-called solitary marriages. There may not be two engaged humans, but there can be—with your initiation alone—two engaged parties: you and God.

Paul promises us that God will give us the will, the work, and even the motivation. As the infomercials like to say, however, "But wait! There's more!"

Shine Like Stars

Paul warns against a huge temptation if we feel we're going it alone: "Do everything without grumbling or arguing" (Phil. 2:14). Grumbling is the opposite of divine dependence. It signifies a focus on where our spouses fall short rather than on God and how richly He provides. It tempts us to try to work it out with a human without first praying it out with our God.

If we instead turn toward divine dependence and then succeed in this endeavor of letting God give us the will and the work for His good pleasure, the result will be spectacular: "'In a warped and crooked generation' … you will shine among them like stars in the sky" (Phil. 2:15).

When other marriages succumb to the perversities of a crooked generation, while our neighbors try to "spice up" their marriages with things that are offensive to God and short-term boosts of romance at best, when others let their passion seep out of their homes year by year through willful neglect, God's children—those truly dependent on and devoted to Him—will shine like stars on a dark night.

What a glorious reality. Even better, the whole Philippians 2:12–15 passage suggests that this doesn't depend on us. Let God give you both the will and the work, for His good pleasure, until you shine like stars in a dark and crooked generation.

Building a Lifelong Love

1. Do you believe you care about your marriage more than your spouse does? If so, what are two or three takeaways from this chapter that can help you spiritually and relationally?
2. Have you taken your spouse for granted by letting things outside your marriage take precedence over your marriage? If so, I want to encourage you to prayerfully consider making the changes necessary to be true to your wedding vows and then to share those changes with your spouse.
3. Is there any area of vulnerability on the part of your spouse—things he or she needs or desires from you—that you are being callous toward? If so, what is it? What can you do to make a change? Do you need to talk to someone outside your marriage who will hold you accountable?
4. Have you been asking God for the will and the work, or have you been struggling on your own? If this has been a weakness, type out Philippians 2:12–15 and post it on your bedroom or bathroom mirror. Commit the passage to memory.

Our loving Father, we sometimes set our sights so low. We want a momentary reprieve from our miseries, while You want us to "shine like stars" in a dark and crooked world. Convince us that You desire the transformation of our marriage even more than we do. Empower us to be faithful in our actions even if my spouse remains distant. Guard our hearts from murmuring or complaining. Grant us the humility to depend on You for both the will and the work that we need in our marriage. In Jesus's name, amen.

15

How One Couple Rescued a "Love Lost" Marriage

If it is true that a good marriage isn't something you find but something you make, then it is also true that a broken marriage can be remade. This is particularly true for believers who hope in the God who proclaimed, "Again I will build you and you will be rebuilt" (Jer. 31:4 NASB). I love the way my friend, pastor and author Ted Cunningham, put this: "Jesus breathes life into dead people, and I believe He breathes life into dead marriages."

If your "journey toward each other" has taken you away from each other, you can build a road back together. Many have. In this chapter, I want to feature one such couple as a

stroke has brought us back!

practical example of how a completely broken marriage can gradually turn around and find intimacy again.*

Megan Raines and her husband thought their marriage was at an end. They even began speaking about divorce. It was the common downward drift, at a very common time in their marriage, that has slain so many couples.

I'm going to let Megan speak first person. Her voice captures both the hurt and the hope and offers a genuine testimony of a love-regained marriage. I have purposefully not edited out some parts I would be inclined to (including a mention of one of my books), because this is *her* story, and I want to honor that.

> Two years ago my marriage was failing. To say it was shaky doesn't even come close. It was literally falling apart day by day. Living in the same house but barely speaking.
>
> Simple questions turning into intense yelling matches.
>
> Zero intimacy physically or emotionally.
>
> Sleeping in separate rooms.
>
> This was not how I was raised to view marriage, nor did I ever believe it would happen to me.

---

* Megan blogs at http://meganraines.wordpress.com. If you want a book-length story of a couple who got remarried after divorce, I love Cheryl and Jeff Scruggs's *I Do Again*.

Then it happened. The big "D" word, "divorce," was thrown out there. Both of us were so miserable we were actually considering it. Neither of us believed in it, but we didn't see any better option. We thought what the world tells us must be true: "*Get out while you still can.*"

Then we found out we were pregnant with our second child. We hadn't been intimate in months, but, apparently, one time (that seemed so long ago) was all it took. Clearly, God had other plans. This baby would be the beginning to a greater plan God had for us and our marriage.

Things didn't immediately get better. In fact, they got worse. For a while I hated being pregnant. I felt as though I was now "stuck" with him. Those feelings and my actions towards him in turn only made him angry and dislike me more. But we knew for the sake of our children we needed to figure something out. Where did our "marriage recovery" start?

First, it began with **prayer**. We spent so much time alone and together in prayer, daily seeking the Lord's will for both of us as a couple, for us as parents, and for us as individuals.

Next, it carried forward with **communication**. We started trying to communicate better and to resolve issues differently than before. I learned how the way I chose to respond to him would influence his reaction, which would ultimately be the deciding factor on the next five minutes of either laughing at our dumb disagreement or blowing up into a yelling match. And he in turn was doing the same with his responses.

Three, we started receiving **godly counsel**. I began seeing a counselor for myself. Fighting the battle of fixing our marriage, being a stay at home mom, and the emotions of being pregnant followed by postpartum issues and dealing with some other family problems on my side of the family, I knew I needed someone other than my husband or friends to talk to. It made a world of difference. The counselor just listened. And because they were Christian, they could scripturally give me advice without telling me what I needed to do or didn't need to do. The best advice I ever got was *"The most important thing you can give your kids isn't a perfect marriage; it's a healthy mom."* I needed to work on *me*. So that's what I did. And boy did we ever see a change in things once I did. (Due to his work schedule my husband wasn't able to see someone, but he spoke often with an accountability partner on the phone and he was making changes too.)

Four, we bought some **couple devotions** and got in **the Word** together. It was so helpful to have something that he and I could do *together* at night before bed, in the quiet of our bedroom, free from any disturbance. They really helped. One of them each night had us both getting very deep and open with one another. We had to ask questions and answer them with painful honesty. Walls were coming down and God was healing our marriage.

Five—and this is a big one—I stumbled upon an amazing book, *Sacred Marriage* by Gary Thomas. This book changed our marriage radically. It opened our eyes to how much trials and stumbling blocks and disagreements could actually make our weak areas stronger and actually draw us closer to God and make us more Christ-like. We began to take a completely different approach to how we worked apart and as a couple. I'm not saying that book is for everyone, but finding material that fits your situation and can help that is scripturally based is a huge tool!

Fast-forward two years, and where are we at today? Well we are *still* together, happily married. In fact we are more in love with not just one another than ever, but also God. As we both dove deeper into knowing Him, and growing in Him, we began doing the same with one another. The "triangle" theory was actually becoming truth. "As two people move closer to God on their own tracks, they move closer together." I have never loved someone so much in my life. He is the man of my dreams and my helpmate. Does this mean everything is perfect? By no means, but it does mean we now have a healthier, godly approach to our differences or "bad days" (which are now very far and few between, praise the Lord) instead of the worldly "dump and run away" approach.

We are also working towards a ministry together as well as both of us having our own ministries and callings, and both have a heart to help other couples never get to where we got, and if they are already there, help them get through it.

And that precious baby? Well we found out she was a girl, and after much prayer named her Cadia. Her name is from Arcadia which means "place of peace; place where fears and trials are released." And she did just that. That little baby girl changed our marriage for the better, and she is such a special edition to our lives! I no longer am bitter, but instead praise God daily for the pregnancy which began the road to save my marriage. God knew what he was doing with that little girl. In fact he was probably laughing to himself the day we found out we were pregnant. Big smile on his face! His sense of humor no longer surprises me. I embrace it.

Now for you, I encourage you, when the waters get rough, and they will, because that's life, don't run away from each other, don't hide, don't shut down. Instead run to God. Open yourself up to one another and to him. I have learned that nine times out of ten it's not actually my spouse that I'm annoyed or upset with. It's actually a deeper issue that needs to be resolved between me and myself or me and God, and something my husband says or does just becomes "the straw that breaks the camel's back."

And my most important, last suggestion? **PRAY.** Pray like your life and marriage depend on it, because oddly enough, they do! The road may be long and bumpy, but when you get to the other side and can step back and look at all God did and will continue doing, all those bumps are so worth it. This is a new year and one of my resolutions was to discover new ways to love and adore and bless my husband, because I want to be 60 and still finding out something new every day about him and still falling madly in love with him day after day!

May the Lord greatly bless you, and bless your marriage as you begin your journey to restoration! And when the waters seem too rough, remember

… you have a life raft. Jesus Christ. And with one word, he can calm the seas. **"Peace."** Trust me: that's exactly where you want to be, in his perfect **PEACE**.[1]

A Good Marriage Is a Good Marriage

You can see that Megan and her husband didn't find a buried secret. They just persistently applied some common truth and slowly began to put their marriage back together, growing toward God and then growing toward each other. They will have to keep this up if they want to keep growing together. If they ever go back to the old patterns, the old feelings and the old alienation will return. That's true for every one of us.

Most of us, like Megan, are evaluating our marriages on a regular basis. We may not even realize we're doing it, but these unspoken thoughts shape our feelings and our contentment regarding our relationships.

Voltaire, a famous writer from the French Enlightenment, warned us not to let the perfect become the enemy of the good. That's not a bad motto for marriage, in this sense: Can we call a good marriage a "good" marriage, or in your mind is that a "bad" marriage? Some people seem to think unless they have a *perfect* marriage, they have a "bad" marriage. They won't put up with a "good" marriage; they want something even better.

If we take our agenda from Matthew 6:33, however, we know that fulfillment comes from outside of marriage. So a good marriage can be a pleasant place to live. If the only thing I have to live for is my marriage, I could imagine not being willing to put up with a good marriage. I might think I need to reach for a superextraordinary one and if I don't reach it, I'll end up resentful or divorcing my spouse in pursuit of a more perfect union. Such disappointment and hyperexpectations are behind many marital breakups.

Every marriage will ultimately reach that point when the spouses finally realize that no human relationship can be ultimately fulfilling. In one sense, this can be a holy moment, a divine disillusionment when we realize that, as amazing as marriage is, we were made for more. Spiritual maturity is found when we can respond to that disillusionment by saying, "This is a good marriage. Given all the other loves I have, with my children, my friends, my walk with God, my soul is overflowing with gratitude, even if my marriage never gets 'better' than it is right now."

In other words, instead of pounding our marriage for what it's not, we rejoice in what it is. We call a good marriage a good marriage, a mission-based partnership with some very pleasurable fringe benefits! "O magnify the LORD with me, and let us exalt His name together" (Ps. 34:3 NASB).

This is a passion worthy of basing your marriage on. It is a passion that can grow in its intensity. It is a passion that is sustained by God instead of by our emotions. It is a passion that sets us up for eternity instead of just a date night. It is a passion that can take a seemingly dead marriage and bring it back to life. Why not give it a try?

Building a Lifelong Love

1. Is there a worst moment in your marriage you can look back on? Perhaps it was a time when, like Megan, you even began contemplating divorce. What do you think led up to that season? What kept you together?

2. Do you agree with Megan that it is possible for two people who seem estranged and frustrated with each other as spouses to become intimate partners once again? Why do you think our "default" way of thinking is that changing partners rather than changing the way we act toward each other best solves misery?

3. Megan offered five practices that helped her and her husband grow back together again. Would you add anything to those five steps? What would you recommend to a couple facing possible estrangement?

4. Do you agree that a "good" marriage is enough for a good life, or do you believe marriage must be extraordinary? Do you know any such marriages? How do we walk the fine line of wanting our marriages to go deeper while still being thankful for the marriages that we have?

Jehovah Rapha, God our healer, please gather into Your arms all couples who feel estranged from each other. Let us feed upon the hope that You can put right what we have destroyed. You can rebuild what we have torn down. You can give new birth to a marriage that we have rejected. Speak practical truths into our minds this very moment—what two or three things would You have us practice to renew our love? Help us to place our marriage in its appropriate context—neither asking too much of our marriage, nor settling for too little. We pray in Jesus's name, amen.

Part Three

The Journey
Toward Love

The Most Important Thing

There were those on my high school track team who just hated doing intervals. Intervals are intense workouts, at high speed, of shorter distances, designed to increase your anaerobic capacity—to make you faster. Some of my teammates didn't mind the long, slow runs where they could laugh, tell stories, and joke around. But the intervals, around the track, in full sight of the coach—not so much.

I liked doing intervals. They hurt, but they fed right into my latent OCD-ness. (I've said in public that while I might not be diagnosed with OCD, I live in the neighborhood right next door to it.)

The reason intervals are essential for track athletes is that every footrace is all about going fast. In the end, that's all that matters. Whether you go fast for 100 meters or 26.2 miles, all that is judged is how quickly you can finish the race. They don't judge your form. They don't add or deduct points for your uniform. They don't care whether you look like a gazelle or a gorilla. All they care about is who crosses the line first.

Christian ethics have a similar "this is all that really matters" element. Every New Testament ethic—beginning with Jesus, going through Paul, bringing in Peter and certainly John—exalts love.

Jesus called love for others an essential element of the greatest commandment (Matt. 22:37–40). John said that if we don't love, we're not believers (1 John 4:7–8). He didn't say if you look at pornography, you're not a believer; or if you gossip, you're not a believer; or if you get drunk now and then, you're not a believer. He *did* say, "If you don't love, you don't know Christ."

Peter likewise saw love as the essential element of Christian being: "Now that you have purified your souls by your obedience to the truth so that you have genuine mutual love, love one another deeply from the heart" (1 Pet. 1:22 NRSV).

We like to focus on individual points of piety ("How far is too far when it comes to dating?" "Should Christians smoke?" "What's worse—gambling or gluttony?"), but the New Testament ethic puts piety on a level of "Are you loving others?" Now, of course, supporting a porn industry that enslaves, demeans, and even traffics women is not love. Gossiping about others—tearing them down socially—is an assault on love. Getting drunk means you are far more likely to act stupidly toward someone—or even kill them, if you drive—so it, too, is not an acceptable act for Christians. But the main element of these sins is that they keep us from doing what matters most: love.

For Christians, a weak, lukewarm love is not enough. We are to become a people who excel not just at loving but at loving *deeply*, from the heart. And marriage can teach us to do just that.

If you pray but don't love, according to Paul, you are nothing (1 Cor. 13). If you know the Bible better than anyone else in your house and your church, but you love others the least, you are the most immature believer in your house or church.

It is all about love.

Let's go back to 1 Peter: we are to love one another deeply. Think about how you love your spouse. It's not enough to avoid doing him or her harm. It's not enough to occasionally be kind and thoughtful. It's not enough to make your spouse feel special on his or her birthday or on Valentine's Day. Are you loving your spouse deeply? If I were to ask your spouse, "Are you deeply loved by your husband/wife?" what would he or she say?

In track, I could wear the cleanest shoes, I could run the most miles, I could work on having the perfect running form, but in the end, the only thing that matters is whether I can run faster than anyone else at my chosen distance.

That same sort of focus is true in Christian faith and Christian marriage. All that matters, in the end, is love. That's because if we love, everything else is taken care of.

So how are you doing when it comes to love? Do you love deeply? Are you excelling at love? To the extent we're not, we're failing at marriage.

This is the third leg of the stool of a truly sacred marriage, necessary to build a lifelong love.

16

Our Greatest Need

As a runner, I've grown to loathe spiderwebs. I've inadvertently sucked in and eaten more than my fair share, or had to pull their sticky swaths off my sweaty body and out of my hair. Even worse, I hate the concept of a spiderweb—the product of an insect that literally seeks to trap passersby, pulling them all into its own world in order to consume them.

Some spouses are like that. They construct marital webs by attracting spouses they think will meet their needs. They "feed" off their spouses whenever they are hungry (for approval, sex, support, finances). Spiders don't give to anyone. They spend their lives creating traps and feeding off anything they catch.

Some people, in retrospect, will blatantly confess they married as a spider.

"I knew he'd put me through medical school."

"I couldn't wait to have sex, and she was willing to marry me, so ..."

"My kids needed a dad, and he seemed like he'd be a good one."

"I needed to get out of my parents' house, and he was offering a quick exit. I thought it would just get my parents off my back."

"I'm an addict, and she's a helper. I thought I'd eventually destroy myself if she wasn't watching me all the time."

It's easy to slip into being a spider spouse, even after the wedding—it doesn't sound so evil to expect another person to live for us when we couch it in romantic language. And the fact that the other person, in the throes of infatuation, may *have* practically lived for us gives us some credence that sometimes it happens, so why should it ever end?

For a Christian, however, our highest desires for our spouses should be to want them to seek first the kingdom of God, to love God with all their hearts, souls, minds, and strength. Seeking to consume someone in the name of love is a selfish lie.

When you are plotting to get something from your spouse, just know that you're acting like a spider. Certainly, there are legitimate needs in marriage, and it's not wrong to ask for them. But I can't let needs define my marriage or become the focus of my day. I shouldn't—please, God, don't let me—slip into spending more time plotting how I can manipulate my spouse to do what I want her to do than praying to God about how I can love, serve, and support her. Jesus teaches us that it is better to give than to receive.

It took me years to come to the realization that marriage is about loving, giving, serving, encouraging, and helping, in large part because I had an entirely different perspective than God did on what my greatest need was. I had yet to discover just how revolutionary Ephesians 5 could be to a marriage. And I'm not talking about verse 22 ("Wives, submit yourselves to your own husbands") or verse 25 ("Husbands, love your wives, just as Christ loved the church")—the ones usually mentioned about marriage. I'm talking about verses 1–2: "Be imitators of God, therefore, as dearly loved children and live a life of love, just as Christ loved us and gave himself up for us as a fragrant offering and sacrifice to God" (NIV, 1984 printing).

Why Did You Get Married?

Ask yourself a question, but pause before you answer it: Why did you get married?

When this question came to me in prayer, I was shocked at my answer. In God's presence, I couldn't hide. I got married for entirely selfish reasons.

I thought I'd have a better life being married to Lisa than not being married to her (or being married to someone else), so I wanted her to marry me. The way she looked, acted, thought, my view of her potential as a parent—these were all things I wanted. Selfishly so. Yeah, I was a spider spouse.

It was so shocking for me to realize that I had gotten married for primarily selfish reasons, especially because I now understand that God created marriage in part to rid me of my selfishness and pride, to teach me how to live "a life of love." On my wedding day, God and I were trying to achieve two entirely different aims. I wanted to be loved. God wanted me to learn how to love.

In my book for singles, *The Sacred Search*, I urge single people to let Matthew 6:33 and spiritual mission drive their choice of marriage. It is not selfish to want to marry someone who will be a strong prayer partner, a spectacular parent (that's a gift to your future kids), and so on. In fact, I even warn against foolishly "marrying for mercy"; so if you're single and reading this, I'd urge you to consider that teaching before absorbing this one. Talking to people who are already married, however, necessitates a call for a realignment in our thinking.

No one has challenged me when I suggest in front of large groups that virtually all of us get married for selfish reasons. It's understandable. But we have to get over this if we want to move into a sacred marriage. That begins with understanding our greatest need from God's perspective.

180 Degrees

One hundred eighty degrees is how hot I like my chai tea lattes, and it's also the difference between what I initially thought my greatest need in life was compared to what God thinks.

Most of us, I believe, are eager to get married because we think our greatest need is to be loved. We want to find someone who will always have our backs, who will be 100 percent faithful, who will be there whenever we need them to be, who will never falter in their love, who will forgive us when we falter in ours, and who will stay with us until the very end.

Pause for just a minute. Who does that sound like, really? Is it possible for a person to do that? It's what we thirst for, however: "What a person desires is unfailing love" (Prov. 19:22). But the Bible tells us it's also elusive: "Many claim to have unfailing love, but a faithful person who can find?" (Prov. 20:6). In the end, there's only one place we'll find it, and it's not in marriage: "I [God] lavish unfailing love for a thousand generations on those who love me" (Exod. 20:6 NLT).

Infatuation can make us feel like we might have found unfailing love in a spouse, but eventually life will prove that a person can't love us like that. Then we feel cheated and misled.

From God's perspective, our greatest need isn't to be loved, not because we don't need to be loved, but in the same way that a person who has just feasted at Thanksgiving doesn't need to eat. God has loved, is loving, and will love us like we can never be loved by anyone else. We may not experience that love in a personal way if we are not making our relationship with God a priority, but it is there for the taking. God isn't hiding from us.

Which means my greatest need, and your greatest need, isn't to be loved (because that need has already been met by God). Our greatest need is to learn *how* to love.

That's the key behind Ephesians 5:1–2. Because we are God's "dearly loved children," our need to be loved has been met, and now we are to imitate God by (I just love this phrase) "living a life of love," just as Christ loved us and gave Himself up for us. God has done (and is doing) His part—He has loved us, and He keeps loving us. And, as *dearly* loved children, we can now focus on the all-important task of "living a life of love."

In Colossians 3:14, Paul wrote, "Above all, clothe yourselves with love, which binds everything together in perfect harmony" (NRSV). In his first epistle, Peter used nearly the same language, demonstrating that this was a common teaching in the early church: "Above all, maintain constant love for one another, for love covers a multitude of sins" (4:8 NRSV).

In 1 Corinthians 13, Paul couldn't have been more intense: "If I have prophetic powers, and understand all mysteries and all knowledge, and if I have all faith, so as to remove mountains, but do not have love, I am nothing. If I give away all my possessions, and if I hand over my body so that I may boast, but do not have love, I gain nothing" (vv. 2–3 NRSV).

Love, love, love. Two different biblical authors saying, "Above all, love." Jesus declaring love as an essential element of the greatest commandment. God could not make Himself heard more clearly. He wants us to learn how to love.

Few things will be as revolutionary in your marriage as accepting that your greatest need isn't to be loved but to learn how to love—not love Hollywood style, but love the way Jesus loved, the way the apostle Paul defined love. I challenge anyone to study the biblical exaltation of love, the sacrificial definition of love, and the imperative to keep loving and then tell me, "Don't worry, Gary, I've got love down pat. I'm ready for the next lesson."

When I think my greatest need is to be loved and I'm not being loved by my spouse as I think I need to be, I become bitter and resentful. When I honestly believe that I need to learn how to love, when I aspire to live a life of love above all else, *every day* of marriage provides ample opportunities for me to grow in that need, which means I will appreciate my marriage more and more. How much I accept this—my greatest need—will determine in large part my overall satisfaction in marriage. Show me a person who thinks his greatest need is to be loved, and I'll show you a person who often wonders if he married the wrong person. Show me a person who truly aspires to live a life of love, and I guarantee she is more contented in her marriage than the average spouse.

The Call to Love

First John 3:11 says that the message we heard "from the beginning" is that we should love each other. The *beginning* of God's message to us is that we need to learn how to love. John then tells us how to love ("not with words or speech but with actions and in truth") in verse 18, and he states that Jesus's commandment is that we love each other in verse 23.

Paul commands husbands to love their wives as Christ loves the church in Ephesians 5:25–26, and in Colossians 3:19 he repeats himself: "Husbands, love your wives and never treat them harshly" (NRSV). Paul can hardly mention marriage without exhorting men to love. He's telling us, "Men, excel in love! Don't forget to love! Focus on growing in love." How many of us men truly view our marriages as places where we must be exhorted to grow in the all-important ("above all") art of learning how to love?

Paul's not silent with women either, telling older women to train younger women how to love their husbands (Titus 2:4). Paul is telling Titus to set up churches that all but organize schools for young wives to excel in the art of loving their husbands. The assumption is that young wives need training to learn how to do this. That's not a surprise—love doesn't come naturally to any of us—but the thought of training wives to love husbands is scandalous to many modern minds.

For both men and women, our ability to love isn't something we master—it's a journey we begin. Paul commends the Thessalonians because "the love of every one of you for one another *is increasing*" (2 Thess. 1:3 NRSV). I should be more loving today than I was five years ago, far more motivated by love today than I was a decade ago, and hopefully much more loving five years from now than I am today. I need to keep working at love, which is why marriage is so tailor-made to help us grow in our greatest need.

Now, show me *one verse* where the Bible says in order to live a successful life I must find one person who will love me unconditionally. Show me even one passage where the Bible says I will be incomplete until I find another human being to always have my back. Yes, God told Adam it wasn't good for him to be alone, I'll give you that one, but when we look at the exhortation passages of Scripture, we are never told that our focus is to find someone to love us. We are always told that our focus is to grow in our capacity and willingness to love others, to live a life of love.

The Bible doesn't tell me, time after time after time, to make sure I drink when I'm thirsty, because that is natural to me. Its overwhelming teaching—almost over the top when you think about it—on our desperate need to become people marked by love testifies to how unnatural this truth is to all of us and why we need the supernatural fruit of the Spirit to die to our narcissism and selfishness.

Peter urges us to "live for the rest of your earthly life no longer by human desires but by the will of God" (1 Pet. 4:2 NRSV). God's will is that we love; 90 percent of human desires consist of wanting to be loved. Marriage can train us to make this all-important shift, provided we look at our marriages as a school to love and provided we value the opportunity to grow in love. *We won't value the opportunity, however, if we don't see it as a need.*

She Asked a Question

In her marvelous book, which I highly recommend, *What's It Like to Be Married to Me?*, Linda Dillow told the true story of a military wife whose husband served as a brigade surgeon in Iraq. When he received notice six months after being deployed that he was about to get a two-week leave, he emailed his wife, Krista, whose first thoughts were along the lines of *Fantastic! I've been a single mom for six months, but now is my chance to have someone else watch the kids while I go to the spa and reengage with some friends.*

That was her initial inclination, but it was not the final one. Though not using this language, she started thinking, *What if my greatest need isn't to be loved but to learn how to love? How would that affect this situation?* She found herself praying, "How can I fill up my husband, spirit, soul, and body, so that he can go back to war for six more months?"

That was a prayer to which she believed God gave her some very practical ideas:

- She wrote Caleb and asked him everything he wanted to eat for two weeks.
- She bought seven bedroom outfits in seven different colors.
- She arranged child care with a friend so she and Caleb could have twenty-four hours alone with each other.
- She bought a massage book and studied it.

After greeting Caleb at the airport, she and the kids took him out to dinner. Krista then made sure the kids were taken care of, and knowing that Caleb's love language is physical touch, they "made out—just because we could!"

She then went into the bathroom and drew Caleb a bath. The account is so touching I'll let her describe it in her own words:

> I straddled the tub with my big sponge and began to cleanse the smells of war. And as I washed the odor of war away, I prayed to cleanse his soul from the spirit of death and destruction. As

> I washed his head and hair, I prayed, *Lord, let nothing he has thought harm him.* As I wiped his eyes, I prayed, *Lord, let nothing he has seen stay in his heart.* As I washed his ears, I prayed, *Lord, let nothing he has heard touch his spirit.* I washed and prayed over every part of my husband, begging God that nothing would take root, that all evil would be washed away.

This was a very spiritual moment, literally praying for and all but anointing every part of her husband's body, pleading with God to bring healing and restoration. A very spiritual moment indeed.

Then it became very physical.

Krista climbed into the bath with him and said, "Honey, pick a color."

Caleb was understandably confused.

"Just pick one ... you'll be glad you did."

Caleb finally chose one, and Krista climbed out of the tub and in just a few moments came back into the bathroom wearing one of the bedroom outfits that was exactly the color Caleb had chosen. In Krista's words, "We made love five times in the first twenty-four hours he was home.... Was this even physically possible?" (I'm not sure; that may take military training.)

A few days later, Krista put her new massage techniques into practice. Caleb became so relaxed during the massage that he slept for two hours straight and woke up saying, "That was amazing. I never slept like that once in Iraq."

Caleb did offer Krista some time to catch up on things, but her focus was on her husband—which seems astonishing to me. I get how a young mother raising kids on her own would want to take advantage of her spouse being home. But looking at her greatest need through this new lens created an experience that I think most wives would consider "legendary."

Listen to this: "Our two weeks were a supernatural feast of intimacy with the Lord and with one another."

How many of you wives would say you and your husband have ever shared a "supernatural feast of intimacy"? This is such an amazing expression, even more surprising in that it was born out of service, humility, and generosity, instead of cleverness, sexual gimmicks, and selfish demands.

Krista went on, "Had I loved him, spirit, soul, and body, so he was ready to return to war? Three days after he got back, he emailed me and said, 'Thank you for the best two weeks of my life.'"[1]

Once again, let me reiterate that I could imagine that any woman in Krista's situation would think, *Now it's my turn; finally, I get a break. Now someone takes care of me.* But Krista didn't go with the natural; she chose the supernatural. She brought God into her marriage by asking how she could love instead of focusing on how she wanted to be loved, and the results were, in her words, "a supernatural feast of intimacy."

Will you accept that your greatest need—to be fully known and loved—can be met completely only by God? And will you then accept that your greatest need now, with the comfort of that love, is to learn how to love?

If you will, I believe your marriage will take you to a depth of spiritual intimacy and even spiritual satisfaction that is unrivaled.

"I give you a new commandment, that you love one another. Just as I have loved you, you also should love one another. By this everyone will know that you are my disciples, if you have love for one another" (John 13:34–35 NRSV).

Building a Lifelong Love

1. Think back to your engagement day. What was your primary motivation to get married? How has believing that your primary need is to be loved assaulted your satisfaction in marriage? Made life difficult for your spouse?

2. Have you ever consciously thought about improving in the art of "living a life of love?" What two things do you think you need to begin doing to start (or continue) on that journey?

3. Think of a situation in your marriage right now where you can easily be stretched to love in a way you never have before. Will you accept the challenge, pray about your heart and actions, and grow accordingly?

4. How can you become a Krista to your spouse in whatever he or she is going through?

O God of love, let us know just how deeply You love us. You call us Your "dearly loved children," but sometimes we feel condemnation. We know we can love only because we have first been loved—Your Word tells us that—so wash us with Your love, let Your love overwhelm us, call us deeper into a conscious experience of Your love. Thus renewed, convict us by Your Holy Spirit that our greatest need truly is to learn how to love. Under Your grace, let us see just how selfishly we have acted in our marriage. Help us perceive how miserable we have made each other by our skewed priorities. And then, dear Lord, lead us into a life of love, the life lived by Your Son, the life promised to us by the empowering presence of Your Spirit. In Jesus's name, amen.

17

Absolute Benevolence

What causes you to love your spouse?

Is it her grace?

His kindness?

Her strength?

His humor?

That she's such a good mom? That he's an unusually involved father?

All of these are inferior reasons and inferior loves, if the famous Puritan Jonathan Edwards is to be believed.

Edwards's essay[1] on this is classically academic, so I'm not even going to try to quote it, as I would put some of you to sleep if I did. Let me restate it so that someone as simple as me can understand it: If you love your spouse because she is kind, you love kindness, not your spouse. If you love your spouse because he is thoughtful, you love thoughtfulness, not your spouse. True love is found in absolute benevolence, which is a state of the heart that is bent toward loving someone's highest good, regardless of the person's actions or character. It is a disposition to do what is best for the other, out of the inner compulsion from the Holy Spirit, to serve this person's best interests.

I want to repeat this sentence one more time so that it's clear what we're talking about when we keep referring to "love": *Love is a disposition to do what is best for the other, out of the inner compulsion from the Holy Spirit, to serve this person's best interests.*

You'll remember the verse that Christ died for us while we were yet sinners (Rom. 5:8). He didn't love us because we were obedient or kind or thoughtful; He loved us with an absolute benevolence that will sound like a tautology: He loved us because He loves us. There is no explanation for this love. Someone objectively examining it could only conclude, "Why did God choose to love *him*? Why does God choose to love *her*? It makes no sense."

What this means, men, is that when I'm called to love my wife like Christ loves the church (Eph. 5:25), I'm called to love her with absolute benevolence. To model such a love, we need to love so benevolently that onlookers might say, "Wow, he really loves her. Why would a man love a woman *that much*?"

As married people, we are invited to adopt an attitude of absolute benevolence toward our spouses—always wanting what is best for them. My good friend Dr. Steve Wilke put the bar very, very high when he defined marital abuse as "any non-nurturing behavior." Love is always set on the beloved's welfare—so all our actions should be motivated for their good. *All* our actions. Every one.

How do we get there? Is this even realistic? Big attitudes can be shaped through little actions. When we were visiting the Seattle area on a recent Thanksgiving, it was, surprise, surprise, raining! Lisa grew up in the Pacific Northwest, but she's been in Houston for more than three years. My only thought was to get her in my parents' house as quickly as possible. I got out of the car and opened up the back to get my suitcase, then closed it.

Lisa was a couple of steps behind me. "If you open it back up, I can get mine," she said.

Lisa hates moving suitcases; she was just being kind. "Don't worry; I've got it," I said. "Besides, it's raining."

"But that means you'll have to go out in the rain *twice* to bring in mine."

What she was saying was logical, but I wasn't looking at the situation logically. I was trying to look at it, in one sense, biblically.* There are a thousand and one ways I could improve on being a husband, but in this instance, my concern really was solely focused on Lisa—how could I best serve her? She doesn't like to lift suitcases and she's not a fan of getting her hair wet before a family dinner. How long I was going to be in the rain wasn't even on my radar. I just didn't want her to have to do something I know she really doesn't like to do.

---

* I am not pitting the Bible against logic! Please read this in context.

That's such a small, insignificant example, but small moments can become habits, and habits shape character. If we aspire to absolute benevolence, then we have to look at such common life situations and ask, "How can I bless my wife here?" A disposition to always do what is best for the other, out of the inner compulsion from the Holy Spirit, is absolute benevolence in simple language.

Prevailing Love

Absolute benevolence is another way of describing *prevailing* love or *lifelong* love. If I love my spouse because I love my spouse, I don't love her because she's healthy or young or beautiful or wealthy or godly or because she has given me a family; so I won't stop loving her if she grows sick or old or becomes disfigured or gets in debt or rebels against God. I'll love her because I love her.

Since marriage calls us to absolute benevolence, an unconditional commitment, it requires nothing less than the presence of God, the only true source of such absolute benevolence. Think about it: Who, on his own, lovingly preaches to people who he knows just want to trap him into saying something for which they can kill him?

Jesus.

Who, on his own, prays for those who are crucifying him?

Jesus.

Who dies for someone who has rebelled against him?

Jesus.

Absolute benevolence is born, then, not just by trying harder but rather by going to God, receiving His love, and passing it on, letting Him transform us so that we love because He first loved us. This might sound overly spiritual, but it's the most practical advice I can give you: if you're not worshipping God daily, you're not loving your spouse with absolute benevolence. We just can't love this way on our own.

A Loving Hand Is a Strong Hand

Now, absolute benevolence does not mean you let your spouse run over you. I received an email from a wife who wondered how to respond when her husband said that part of "accepting" him was accepting that he was an alcoholic and was going to get drunk. Love does not stand by while another person ruins himself.

After all, God loves us—and disciplines us. "When we are judged in this way by the Lord, we are being disciplined so that we will not be finally condemned with the world" (1 Cor. 11:32). God would rather have us walk through shame, pain, the loss of a job, and even worldly humiliation than watch us walk comfortably into hell. He disciplines us for our own good.

A husband and wife I talked to were being ground down by the wife's poorly chosen priorities. The husband had put up with it for too long and his bitterness was palpable. He thought love meant just grinning and bearing it, but that's a short-term strategy at best. The most loving thing he could do was what he eventually did—bring the two of them into a counselor's office where these issues could be addressed. She had a couple of hobbies and a penchant to spend too much time on social media, given their young children. She wanted to be cherished by her husband, but she needed to see that one of the things that would help him cherish her was being willing to reassess her priorities. The Bible describes Christ's love for the church—as an example to husbands—as serving her sanctification (growth in holiness; Eph. 5:26).

Absolute benevolence is the proper passion behind every marital action. If I must separate from my spouse, I will do it, but only because it must be best for her. This is true in the case of, say, abuse. Wives, it's best for your husbands not to hit you; so if the only way you can stop them from doing that is to remove yourselves from their presence, that's what you do. But even that act, from that disposition, is absolute benevolence (though a selfish man will accuse you otherwise).*

This means that to find the right way to act, I simply ask, from God's perspective, what is truly best for my spouse? That tells me what I must will myself to do. I want to do what is best for my spouse. What is best for my spouse? Aha! Then that's what I will do.

How many divorces would be stopped if we loved with absolute benevolence? How many fights would sound ridiculous to resolve in the face of absolute benevolence? How many decisions would be made much easier if we were driven by absolute benevolence?

---

* I say an important word about the church's response to domestic violence in the appendix.

How much would every marriage change if we pursued absolute benevolence over our own comfort, happiness, and self-interest? How many of us, I wonder, will pursue this kind of love, this kind of marriage? Let me assure you, the more you do pursue this, the more your love for your spouse will be renewed. When I love my wife with absolute benevolence, just the sound of her name, the mere thought of her smile, moves me in a way that is difficult to explain.

The more I will to love her with absolute benevolence, the more I cherish her in my heart. Because of God's Spirit in our lives, we can choose to grow in this area, if we fix our minds on the right questions and surrender our wills to God's empowering presence. Ask, "Do I *truly* love my wife for my sake, or her sake? Are my daily actions *confronting* or *confirming* my selfishness?" Let's wake up with these questions every day, offering up our selfish hearts to God and letting Him replace them with the others-centered heart of Jesus, who came not to be served but to serve.

Building a Lifelong Love

1. List several of your favorite things about your spouse. Thank God that He has given you someone with these qualities.
2. This is going to seem a bit artificial, but it'll be helpful. Rate your love for your spouse on this basis: 1 means you love your spouse mostly for what they bring you and who they are, and 10 means you believe you are loving with absolute benevolence (I don't expect to hear of any tens):

1 —— 2 —— 3 —— 4 —— 5 —— 6 —— 7 —— 8 —— 9 —— 10
Love for my sake   Love with absolute benevolence

Sit before God with your answer and let Him lead the conversation about how you can begin loving your spouse with the same love with which God loves you—absolute benevolence.

3. Why do you think a focus on absolute benevolence matters? What do you think it will do to the way you think and feel about your marriage when you pursue this kind of love?

God of heaven, the God who loved us even in our sins, the God who draws us in even in our rebellion yet disciplines us for our good, help us to love each other as we have been loved by You. Let us learn to love as we have never loved before—not for the sake of selfishness but for the sake of each other's good. Let this love renew our feelings and build a relationship that reflects Your character and Your Spirit within us. In Jesus's name, amen.

18

Love Most Glorious

"I guess I still love him, in a way; I'm just not *in* love with him anymore."

How many times have you heard a friend say that about her spouse?

Maybe you've heard *yourself* say that.

Here's a radical thought: Why do we think "in love" love matters more than "biblical love"? Why do we think that, within marriage, whatever we mean by "in love" is the sustaining basis of a lifelong relationship? I love how marriage takes us to the most fundamental of questions, beginning with what we mean by "love" and what we value about love.

When the Bible commands us to love, it says nothing about what we describe as "in love" love. Biblical love isn't a feeling to be felt; it's a commitment to be kept. You can't make yourself feel anything, but you can choose to submit your actions to the will of God. So you can choose to love your spouse if you define love as the Bible does, even if you can't choose to become "in love" once again.

Certainly, "in love" love is a wonderful feeling to be received with thanksgiving, even to celebrate in poetry and songs and novels. And, in the sight of God, if someone asked me today, "Are you in love with your wife?" I would answer, without the slightest hesitation, "Absolutely, yes!" If they followed up with, "Have you two felt that way every minute of the twenty-nine years you've been together?" I'd say, "Not exactly."

God created us with the capacity for feelings of infatuation, and I don't want to deny them or even diminish them below God's creational intention. It's just that, biblically speaking, I'm never commanded—not once!—to "feel" something toward my wife, but I am often commanded to a concept of love that has nothing to do with emotions. So if I want to live biblically, if I want a truly sacred marriage, then I need to aspire after this kind of love (which I can control) without being unduly obsessed about the other kind of love (which I can't control). Let's be clear: a lifelong love doesn't mean a lifelong infatuation.

Love Most Famous

First Corinthians 13 is one of the most famous chapters in the Bible, and rightly so, as it brilliantly defines biblical love. Let's consider just one simple phrase, "love does not boast," and apply that to marriage.

Do you have any idea how often I hear something like this: "Look, I do all the housework, I get the kids where they need to go, I put them to bed, I work a part-time job on top of all of that, and all he does is sit on his rear end as soon as he gets home from his eight-hour-a-day job"?

Now, if I were talking to the husband, I'd have something very different to say. But talking to this wife, if I wanted to apply 1 Corinthians 13, if I wanted to get at her heart before addressing her husband's actions, which is how Jesus consistently seemed to operate, I'd have to say, "You just spent five minutes boasting about how good a spouse you are. But the Bible says love doesn't boast. So maybe you're not as loving a spouse as you think, at least not in biblical terms."

God might well be applauding her actions, but He clearly hates her attitude. If she cares anything at all about worship, she'll lose the boasting. She won't let her right hand know what her left hand is doing when she serves. She'll aspire after a love that delights in serving rather than in boasting resentfully about it.

I had another wife tell me, "When my husband was eighteen, he got fired from Taco Bell for being habitually late. When he was twenty-four, he got kicked out of college for never completing his final course. When he turned thirty, he lost his job because he kept forgetting to answer his phone and was missing too many calls. He's been messing up his whole life."

Maybe so. But she is also radically messing up as a wife, because the Bible says, "Love … keeps no record of wrongs," and she has a pretty long list (I've actually edited it here).

This might sound harsh, but where does the Bible say, "Love your husband *except if he loses a job in college, gets kicked out of college, and is fired for being absentminded*"? I must have missed that verse. But the Bible *does* say, "Love … keeps no record of wrongs."

Yes, both of these marriages have legitimate issues to address. I agree with both wives on that—and, as a pastor, I could envision many long conversations with their respective husbands. I am *not* excusing the husbands' behavior or failings. But what these wives are blind to are the state of their own hearts and the astonishing, radical, biblical definition of love, which means to be so *for* someone (in the way that God is so for us—see Romans 8:31) that it almost sounds absurd. We must become our spouses' biggest champions, even in the midst of their faults, even as God is our biggest champion in the midst of our faults—"But God proves his love for us in that while we still were sinners Christ died for us" (Rom. 5:8 NRSV).

And yet our lack of love in this biblical sense rarely concerns us; many times we're not even aware of our transgressions in this regard. When I call people out on it, using 1 Corinthians 13, they are usually stunned: "I never thought of it like that." Spiritually, they're completely numb to conviction over their biblically described offense to love, yet if any of them suffer a lack of feelings for any significant season, they panic and think something is wrong with their marriages.

Sadly, most spouses are more appalled by their lack of feelings than they are that their actions directly contradict what the Bible defines as loving. If you truly want a lifelong love—and I hope you do—then you must first accept as most important the biblical definition of what love actually is.

To that end, let's go through this list in 1 Corinthians 13 and ask ourselves, "Is this how I love in my marriage?" You are not evaluating your spouse here, because you are not responsible for your spouse in this sense. Let's look at our own hearts. You say you want more "love" in your marriage—well, this is all about building true love.

1. Love is patient. Lisa and I were once driven around Charlotte by a wonderful couple, Lloyd and Pam Bustard. Lloyd is a multiply gifted man, a preacher, pastor, and musician, but it looked like he couldn't drive his way around two city blocks without taking a wrong turn. Yet Pam displayed the most astonishing patience, without any irritation in her voice, that Lisa and I had ever seen. "No, babe, you took a wrong turn there. We have to do a U-turn and go back."

"But I think it's up here."

"No, it's back there.

"Oh, you're right."

There was no growing consternation in Pam's voice. No condescension. Not even a hint of any lack of respect. Multiple mistakes didn't raise any irritation. Pam just sat next to Lloyd and loved him as 1 Corinthians 13 calls us to love. Do you treat your spouse's limitations like Pam treats Lloyd's?

2. Love is kind. What have you done for your spouse lately? Seriously, if you were to list your acts of kindness in the last seven days, how long (or short) would the list be? Have you seen a need and sought to meet it? Have you even considered what active thing you could do for your spouse to show him or her your love and care?

3. Love is not jealous. Do you resent that your spouse gets more consideration from his or her spouse (that is, from you) than you get from yours (that is, from him or her)? That's jealousy! This might sound weird, but I've found it to be relatively common for some spouses to wish they got treated the way they treat their spouses—in a spiritual quirk, they are jealous of their own treatment.

Do you resent that your spouse's role in the family seems easier or better than yours at times? That's jealousy. Real love would be gratified that our spouses have it "better" than we do. Knowing this would delight us rather than make us feel resentful, if we had hearts filled with biblical love.

4. Love does not brag and is not arrogant. How often do you think that you're the "better" spouse? That attitude will keep you from excelling and growing in love and instead foster bitterness and resentment. It'll also turn you into a Pharisee, which means you won't be the "better" spouse for long. Love would never say, "I do this for you, and that for you, I keep on doing x, y, and z, and what do you ever do for me?"

Tell me, what did the disciples ever give to Jesus? How did they give back to Him, proportionally speaking? Would Jesus ever say, "I do miracles for you, I feed you, I pray for you, I teach you all day long, I'm even going to die for you, so what are you going to do for Me?" Remember, we are called to love like Jesus loves. Just think like Jesus would think—would Jesus say to His disciples what you are tempted to say to your spouse?

5. Love does not act unbecomingly. This essentially means being rude. How often do you respond with sarcastic words and attitudes? How do you treat your spouse in public—is your goal to make people pity you for having such a difficult spouse, or is it to proclaim that you treasure your spouse? God treasures you, with all your weaknesses, all your sins. He delights in you. And your sins, known to God, vastly outnumber the sins you are aware of in your spouse. God doesn't act rudely to us, knowing all that He knows. Will we act rudely to our spouses, knowing just what we know?

6. *Love does not seek its own.* Be careful about demanding that your spouse meet your love language or even your respective need for love and respect. These are helpful tools designed to teach you how to love your spouse, but they can be turned around against the authors' intention and used as weapons to accuse your spouse for how he or she is not measuring up. Remember "the two dimensions of marriage" (chapter 13)? What dimension of marriage are you living in?

7. *Love is not provoked.* This kind of love isn't irritable; it doesn't lash out at someone with the least amount of provocation, but rather it remains calm and gentle and seeks to be understanding. It injects calm and collectedness into every situation. It looks out for the triggers of an impending, hurtful argument and says, "I'm not going to take the bait. I'm going to breathe deeply and remain grounded."

8. *Love does not take into account a wrong suffered.* Does your spouse routinely receive grace or judgment? Is your spouse built up with acceptance or weighed down with your disappointment? Is your spouse frequently reminded of how he or she never lives up to your expectations? The goal of biblical love should be that

our spouses are far more aware of what we like about them than they are of what they do or are that frustrates us. Yes, that's a high goal. I'm miles away from it. But that's the goal of true, biblical love.

9. Love does not rejoice in unrighteousness but rejoices with the truth. When you and your spouse disagree, are you more concerned about addressing your contribution to what's wrong or about being proven right? Seek the truth rather than vindication. This also means, however, that when a spouse wants to do something sexually that another spouse has a moral problem with, biblical love doesn't just give in. If a spouse is committing fraud, alienating a child, ruining his or her life, love doesn't mean playing nice and pretending all is well. Love is strong and courageous and speaks what is true, not always what will please.

10. Love bears all things. This means we're called to bear not just some of our spouses' weaknesses but all of them. All of them. That's right—the one that just came into your mind and made you say, "Are you serious?" Yes, I am. That one.

11. Love believes all things and hopes all things. Have you stopped believing for your spouse? Have you stopped dreaming of how God can be fully known and revealed in your spouse's life? Have you given up hope for your spouse—to such an extent that you even tell your spouse in person that you know he or she is just going to fail again? Do you have hope that your spouse can become all that God created him or her to be? To give up hope in your spouse is to give up hope *in God* and His ability to change someone's heart. It's a monstrous thing to do.

12. Love endures all things. There's that phrase "all things" again. Love endures all things. Whatever my spouse puts me through, whatever life leads me through, my call in love is to endure. "Endures" assumes that the problem is ongoing and isn't immediately fixed. "All things" means that, whatever the ongoing challenge, my goal is to build a marriage worthy of my calling. If I'm running a marathon and it starts to rain, I endure the rain. If there are hills, I endure the hills. If it gets hot and humid, I endure the heat and humidity. If my legs cramp, I endure the cramps. Whatever it takes to get to the finish line, that's what I endure. That's biblical love in marriage.

13. Love never fails. Of course not! If we love like 1 Corinthians 13 has just told us to, how could our love possibly fail? Our spouses may not change, and our marriages may not survive—the Bible doesn't promise that everything will be "fixed"—but what we are to focus on is that our *love* doesn't fail. If you are married to a habitually unfaithful spouse, a drug addict, someone who gets physically violent, a spouse who is mentally ill and refuses to take medication, your marriage may not survive. But that doesn't mean your love has failed. You can keep loving your spouse, as Christ loves us, even as your spouse destroys your marriage. You may have to let your spouse go, as Christ let rebellious sinners go. But that isn't a failure of love—it's an expression of love.

Notice not once does the Bible say, "Love feels intensely." Let's stop worrying about how we feel and start considering how we love, Jesus style. If we honestly measure our hearts by the truth of this passage, we won't have time to worry about feelings. We'll be consumed with building a life of substance.

Pulling Tubes

Having just heard me speak on marriage, the sixty-something woman was already in tears by the time she inched to the front of the line. She had a story to tell, and she kept wiping away the tears until she could tell it.

"What you're saying is so true," she began and then paused to contain herself. "I've worked at a hospice for twenty years. Caring for people is what I do. Yet somehow, it never got transferred to home. I resented doing the very things for my husband that I spent my whole day doing for others."

After another pause, she went on. "Until, that is, my husband got cancer. After the first operation, he stayed home for six weeks, and I stayed with him. It was the best season of marriage we've ever had."

Think about this: she could have chosen the honeymoon, the young years when they were strong and vibrant, the exciting years when occupations opened up, the tired but thrilling years when the kids arrived. So many highlights to choose from, yet this woman chose the season of her husband's *cancer* as the best season of marriage they had ever had.

Why?

"Pulling tubes, cleaning sutures—I'm a nurse, I can do all that—I finally began doing for him everything I've done for everyone else, but I had never served my husband like that the entire time we were married. But now I was. It changed my heart. It changed the way I looked at him. And, serving him like that, it just drew us so close together."

Most people think their marriages will improve when their spouses step up. This wife said her marriage improved when *she* stepped up. I've never read a marital book that talks about building romance by pulling medical tubes and cleaning sutures on your partner, but this dear woman had stumbled onto a powerful truth. She entered into love, Jesus style, and she passionately proclaims that it's a glorious love indeed.

You remember Jesus in John 13, at the Last Supper, when Scripture tells us He got up from the table to show His disciples the full extent of His love. And what did He do?

He washed their feet.

That would be one thing—to show His humility and service by washing His followers' feet. But Jesus went one step further and said, "So if I, your Lord and Teacher, have washed your feet, you also ought to wash one another's feet. For I have set you an example, that you also should do as I have done to you" (John 13:14–15 NRSV).

Then there was a promise "If you know these things, you are blessed *if you do them*" (v. 17 NRSV).

Are you serving others more than you serve your spouse? Husbands, it goes without saying here that any sense of chauvinism, any sense that your wives are there primarily to serve you, goes completely against the spirit of what Jesus was saying. When

Paul said to love our wives like Christ loves the church, he was calling us to be the leader in service, not the leader in privilege. Are you leading like that? And wives, do you find yourselves offering nurturing care to others outside the home with a sweet spirit but resenting it when you're offering similar care at your own address?

The purpose of prior chapters in this section was to convince us of our greatest need—to learn how to love. The purpose of the previous chapter, "Absolute Benevolence," and this chapter is to define that love so that we can see how radical it is. Hopefully, out of this understanding, we'll have a new respect and appreciation for our marriages and for the role they can play in helping us become people of love.

Let's be honest about the state of our families and churches: Do people think the church is too full of people who love like this, or do they think such people and churches are rare? Are we so obsessed with how happy we are in our love that we're neglecting to show the world how much of Jesus is in our marriages?

Do you see how powerful the process of marriage can be, how sacred this journey you've undertaken truly is?

We're not done defining love, however. In our journey toward love, we can go even one step further.

Building a Lifelong Love

1. When you think about the state of your heart, what do you evaluate more often: how you feel about your spouse or how well your love matches up with the Bible's call to love? Is there

something you can do to shift your thinking toward being more concerned about biblical love?

2. Is it possible for a spouse to take advantage of another spouse who seeks to love according to 1 Corinthians 13? If so, what would be the most biblical response?

3. Go back over the list given to us in 1 Corinthians 13. Pick two things that you think you need to focus on in the coming weeks.

4. One woman's love was renewed when she began "pulling tubes" for her sick husband. Are there any "tubes" you need to pull in your own marriage—acts of service you've perhaps done for others but have failed to do for your spouse? Sit before the Lord and invite His conviction.

Most high God, our hearts are so stained that if You didn't tell us what love is, we wouldn't even know. We have turned love into something that is practically opposite of what You declare it to be. Renew us today; redefine what we mean when we say we want to grow in our love. Help us to be honest when we look at Your definition of love and evaluate our hearts and actions. Give us the grace to accept Your forgiveness so that we can honestly face where we are weak, and then send us Your Spirit so that we can be empowered to grow in that very same area. In Jesus's name, amen.

19

Love Isn't Desire

One of the greatest misconceptions today among both singles and marrieds is in our understanding of the words *desire* and *love*. The two are not the same, but we think they are. So, when an immature twenty-five-year-old proclaims, "I love her; I really love her!" he may well be speaking with a five-year-old's heart: "I love candy; I really love candy!"

Because he really, really desires her, he thinks he really, really loves her, but the two realities are worlds apart; the words and concepts are not synonyms, though of course they can coexist. As long as we mix up the two, however, we will misunderstand both, and we will never understand what constitutes a truly sacred marriage.

A five-year-old "loves" candy in the sense that he desires it. He wants to eat it. In the same way, an immature twenty-five-year-old says he "loves" a woman because he desires her. He wants to have sex with her, or at least he wants to be around her and he wants her to want him with the same intensity.

The kind of love the Bible calls us to is a love that is focused on others' welfare; our desire is for their good, not our own benefit. When the five-year-old eats the candy, it is destroyed. When the twenty-five-year-old sleeps with a woman he desires but is not married to, he dishonors her. Both cases are examples of consuming, not loving.

We've already seen that biblical love is perhaps best understood with (though not fully defined by) the old-fashioned word *benevolence*. It is wholly others focused. John 15:13 tells us that the greatest love isn't the greatest desire but an act of self-sacrificing benevolence: "Greater love has no one than this: to lay down one's life for one's friends."

When we separate love from desire, we see how silly it sounds when a married woman says, "I love him, but I'm just not *in love* with him anymore." What she means is that she has stopped desiring him in the same way she used to, but in fact, she has it backward. Love is not desire, but love creates desire. The more loving I act toward someone, the more I begin to desire that person. A wayward parent who ignores his kids is capable of astonishing apathy. Many people have sat in my office, recounting their childhoods, saying, "How could my parent *do* such a thing? How can you not want to even see your child when they're growing up?" A large part of the answer is that when we act in an unloving way, we short-circuit our desire. We become harder, colder, and more distant. Parents who love their kids in a practical way can't stop caring. It's impossible. So if you've been an involved, loving parent, no, you can't understand how people could ignore, abuse, or reject their children. The reason is that your acts of love have softened your heart, just as acts of apathy would have hardened it.

In marriage, however, we have this crazy notion that the selfish aspect of desire must come first (I want to be with you; I like the feeling I get when I see you or hear your voice), thinking that such desire is essential to keep acting. In a biblical (and true) view, if there's no love, eventually desire will be extinguished. In a one-night sexual stand, there might be plenty of desire, but there's no love. The two individuals can walk away from each other without even knowing their first names. They don't care. They don't love. They just desired, and now that their desire is quenched, they can walk away from each other as casually as a man who has just finished his steak can walk away from Outback Steakhouse.

Most of the world thinks a marriage is over when we stop desiring. God says our marriages suffer when we stop loving. That's a huge difference. Force yourself to distinguish between the two. In daily actions, in daily commitment, never forget: Love is not desire. Desire is not love. Love is benevolence, wishing and working toward another's good. That's what marriage calls us to.

Love Is Not What My Lover Desires

The fact that desire is not love affects us in another sense: Just because you want me to do something doesn't mean love demands that I do it. Love is not desire. So, if you desire for me to do something that is hurtful to you or others, or hated by God, you can't say, "If you love me, you'll do this for me." It is precisely because I love you that I *can't* do that for you.

Biblical love most decidedly does not call us to become a doormat for a manipulative, evil spouse. It does not mean giving in to an addict, or physical abuse, or illegal behavior. Love is not measured by our willingness to take risks with the law or to excuse self-destructive behavior in the people we love; it is measured by faithfulness to God, which calls us to confront law breaking and self-destructiveness.

Something doesn't even have to be evil to be denied. Mary and Martha wanted Jesus to heal their brother Lazarus before he died. They could well have said, "If You love us, You will come now, before he dies, and heal him." It is because Jesus loved them, however, that He waited until after Lazarus had died, to show them the glory and power of God. He loved them in a way they didn't understand. He loved them enough to let them wallow in their accusation and misunderstanding and ignorance and false sense of righteous indignation. Clearly, the story assumes a real intimacy between Jesus and this family. They could not have expected Him to come if they were simply one of the crowd. They were friends, beloved intimates.

After Lazarus died, Mary and Martha thought that Jesus's love had failed them because He did not do what they had desired Him to do. Jesus showed us that what someone desires of me does not necessarily constitute what love calls me to do. Love is centered on God's purpose, not human desire. Sometimes, love means saying no, even if that makes the person we love feel unloved.

Changing the Goal

Since there is such a spiritual significance in understanding the difference between desire and love, the goal of our marriages must change accordingly. Most couples I talk to think the goal of marriage is to keep desiring each other like they did when they were infatuated. Now, sometimes I do still desire my wife with that intensity, but the constant goal I must really strive for is best expressed by the apostle John: "If we love one another, God lives in us and his love is made complete in us" (1 John 4:12).

This is a sacred marriage! The expression of our love, the commitment of our love, brings God into our marriages, letting His love be complete in our marriages and sustain our marriages. This is more than human desire. It is, quite literally, worship (acknowledging and reveling in His excellence) and surrender (giving way to His presence).

The problem is that so many spouses ask themselves, without realizing that this is what they are asking, "How can I still *desire* a man who is so selfish and unfeeling and arrogant?" "How can I still *desire* a woman who criticizes everything I do and is ashamed to be seen with me in public?"

Good luck with that.

The root of these questions is the assumption that desire is the all-important commodity for a happy, fulfilling marriage. If I can't make myself desire a fallen person who stumbles in many ways (James 3:2), then my marriage must be over.

But that's not the biblical goal. The biblical goal is a shared experience of *God living in us* and *God's love being made complete in us.* I may not desire a wife who doesn't respect me, but I can still act benevolently. I can revel in the love God pours out on me and, out of that abundance, pour it out on others ("We love because He first loved us"). I love the way Dallas Willard put this: "The first great commandment [love of God] makes it possible to fulfill the second [love of others]."[1]

The pursuit of a sacred marriage is the pursuit of God in marriage—seeking to experience His love (not our desire); His presence (not our happiness); His glory (not our selfishness).

To the spiritually blind, this sounds ridiculously absurd, but those who have tasted God's goodness know that God's love overwhelms our own desire; that His presence brings a joy that makes human "happiness" feel like a small shudder in the face of God's earthquake; that God's glory is so much more fulfilling, in every possible way, than our small-minded selfishness.

Here's the trap sacred marriage saves us from: if what you desire can never satisfy, you will never be satisfied, even if you obtain your desire. The world is teeming with disappointed souls who thought they had found their "one true love" and then one day woke up to find that their one true love wasn't very loving for very long. But if you place your hope in God's love, "hope does not disappoint us, because God's love has been poured into our hearts through the Holy Spirit that has been given to us" (Rom. 5:5 NRSV).

We can't sustain desire, but the Bible promises us that God will sustain *love* because He keeps pouring it into our hearts through His Holy Spirit. A marriage based on desire will be like living on a floodplain—sometimes you'll be underwater, and sometimes it'll be bone dry. That's where, quite frankly, most couples exist. On the other hand, a marriage based on God's love is a steady mountain stream for which you never see the source but you also know it will never run out.

So, what will be the source of our marriages: desire that comes and goes, or the spiritual provision of God, which can never run out? Let's begin to really love, not just sit in the shallowness of desire.

Now, a trickier question. How does this relate to sexual desire? Isn't desire a physiological necessity in the bedroom? Well, yes and no. But that question deserves a chapter all its own, which we'll turn to next.

Building a Lifelong Love

1. As you honestly assess your own attitudes in, and thoughts about, your marriage, do you tend to focus more on what you're feeling or how you're loving? How can you improve in this area?
2. Based on what was discussed in this chapter, if you find your desire for your spouse is muted, where should you look, spiritually? How do you think you should respond?
3. What is the most appropriate way for people to say no, in the name of love, to things their spouses desire?
4. Would you say your marriage has been marked by a shared experience of "God living in us and God's love being made complete in us"? What thoughts from earlier in this book might help you to make that happen to a greater extent?

Heavenly Father, our one true desire, transform our hearts and minds so thoroughly that what we long for above all else is You living in us and Your love being made complete in us. When our desire for each other starts to wane, remind us of what really matters, and then lead us into those actions that will reignite appropriate desire. May we live a lifetime of having our desires renewed by loving actions and Your empowering presence. We pray in Jesus's name, amen.

20

Delightful Desire

"Whoa."

Lisa looked at me and shook her head. We had just met with a young couple, not yet married but eager to be, and just as eager to be sexually intimate. The young man was all but dripping with desire, even trying to plot how to move up the marriage by three months, even though doing so would have been a logistical disaster. The young man just couldn't wait. You could have put a towel underneath the table to catch his pheromones and wrung it out by the time he left. Because he was being faithful to the teachings of Scripture, there was no "relief valve" with his fiancée. His palpable desire drove half of the questions he asked us.

"I think it was healthy for you to see that," I told Lisa. When a wife is married to a fifty-year-old man, it's easy to forget what a guy can be like in his twenties.

There was a time in my life when I practically resented the powerful force of sexual desire, in this sense: I knew how vulnerable it made me to my wife. I knew how precariously my integrity dangled over the force of its flame.

And I resented it.

In prayer, I even offered up this aspect of my free will. I thought that perhaps God could cut me a break and magically reprogram my soul so sexual desire would be much tamer, more focused, more easily controlled.

God gently reprimanded me. You see, I was looking at sexual desire through the lens of the fall—as if it came about because of Satan and sin. Intellectually, I would have rejected that, but in my fears, that's how it sometimes felt. Sexual desire was a temptation rather than a tool.

When I began looking at sexual desire through the lens of creation instead of the fall, I realized that it is God's providential will that I be this vulnerable in my relationship with my wife. God knows that without sexual longing, I might grow weaker in my affections for His daughter. I might allow us to slowly drift apart with nothing in the relationship to show me just how far we've drifted, until the day we wake up and can't even see each other over the horizon. He loves His daughter too much to let that happen, so He designed me with hormones that will all but begin to roar if I slumber in my apathy toward His child.

When I finally realized that God created me to desire my wife and to be vulnerable in that desire, I never looked at our sexual relationship in quite the same way.

That's just one small instance in which I've experienced God expanding my outlook on marital sexuality. The older I get and the more I look into it, the more amazed I am at how sex works not just physically but also spiritually and relationally.

The Desire That Heals

Done well, marital sexuality can be a supremely healing experience.

Most of us grow up with various insecurities about our bodies, and the thought that we are wanted, desired, enjoyed, and then pursued sexually (for the right reasons) can do wonders for a beaten-up self-image.

So, yes, picking up from the previous chapter, desire can be a good thing. Desire can be a catalyst for love and healing.

In the Song of Songs, at a time in history when no women would pay to get a tan (because in that day and culture, the lighter the better), an ashamed bride implored her friends, "Don't stare at me because I am dark—the sun has darkened my skin. My brothers were angry with me; they forced me to care for their vineyards, so I couldn't care for myself" (1:6 NLT).

This young woman feared that people were staring at her not because they were impressed but because they couldn't believe she'd let the sun darken her skin. But though she had entered marriage with the image of herself as attracting attention for all the wrong reasons, her husband set her straight, calling her "most beautiful among women" (v. 8 ESV) and repeating, "How beautiful you are, my darling, how beautiful you are! ... Like a lily among the thorns, so is my darling among the maidens" (1:15; 2:2 NASB).

Understanding this passage can reset a man's view of sexuality within marriage. If you cultivated your sexual interest with pornography, you got the idea that sex is all about getting to your own climax. But here it's all about affirming a woman who grew up believing she was lacking something significant in the beauty department. Though others had mocked her, and though she wasn't "classically" beautiful according to the standards of her culture, her husband not only considered her beautiful but the *most* beautiful among women.

When we stop desiring our wives or start desiring other women, marital sexuality becomes yet another chapter in a woman's mental playbook where she thinks that she doesn't quite measure up. One of the most biblical reasons to guard our hearts, men, and to not let our desire for sexual relations fade (when it's physically possible to sustain) is to continue the healing process of our wives' images of themselves as beautiful, desirable women, whether they are twenty-nine, forty-nine, or sixty-nine.

A female Christian blogger recently wrote about how women simply want to be desired passionately, in her words "taken." An excessively soft, "I'm into it tonight if you are, honey, but really I could take it or leave it" won't cut it long-term (though it may be a reality at times).

We won't go far wrong if we think of it like this: "My wife has been hurt her entire life by an insane culture with ridiculous standards of physical beauty that make no sense. In the shelter of our marriage and under the covering of my love, I'm going to work overtime to affirm her, adore her, desire her, pursue her, verbally praise her, and bring healing to her soul. I want to desire her and love her so much that the hurts, taunts, and criticisms of others will become all but invisible in the force of my passion."

In other words, guys, it's not just about our sexual needs; it's about our wives' hurting souls—using our desires to serve theirs. It's about letting our wives relish and even cherish the power their beauty has over us: "You have made my heart beat faster with a single glance of your eyes" (Song 4:9 NASB). It's about the confidence our wives gain when they know they have captured not just our hearts but our eyes and minds as well.

This is a tremendous gift, one a man gives by intention when he guards his heart, mind, and eyes and cultivates (or recultivates, when he strays) a singular attraction to the woman he calls wife.

Desire may not be a problem on the wedding night, but what about ten years or even twenty-five years into the marriage? How does desire fit into a *lifelong* love?

Keeping the Canary Alive

"Gary," the young wife explained to me, "I want to have a rocking sex life with my husband, but he criticizes everything I do. I don't cook right. I don't drive right. I don't raise the kids right. So I know he's also criticizing every move I make in the bedroom. I just can't bear to have another aspect of marriage life where I'm messing up."

This wife wants a great (rocking!) sex life, but she's tired of being criticized. Her coldness toward the marital bed has nothing to do with sex—it has everything to do with what happens outside the bedroom. Her husband won't warm her up by buying a sexual toy, trying out a new move, and certainly not by quoting 1 Corinthians 7. He has to address the relational poison that's killing her desire for physical passion. To put it bluntly, his wife hates being criticized more than she desires having an orgasm.

I look at a lack of sexual desire (though there are often, of course, physical causes that need to be addressed) as that famous "canary in the mine." Old-time miners used to keep canaries down in the depths of the mines. The tiny birds' lungs were so small that if relatively odorless poisonous gas seeped out of the ground, the canaries would die first, and quickly, warning the miners to get out of the mine and into fresh air. In the same way, when sexual desire dies absent of physical causes, it's often indicative that there are relational "poisons" in the home. These toxins may not have killed the marriage yet, but they're making it sick, and the couple needs fresh air.

Sex is an easy measuring stick. If you ask a couple, "When was the last time you made love?" *and they don't know,* that's a big tell.

The early days of sexual passion can be easy, just as "feeling in love" is easy when we're infatuated. Sexual chemistry is high, everything is new, and you can't get enough of each other. But maintaining this sexual interest is another challenge altogether. I've heard many times the cliché phrase that if a married couple puts a marble in a jar every time they have sex for the first two years of their marriage and then take one marble out every time they have sex following that, the jar will never empty. First, I don't believe this is always true, but it probably is often true, which I find to be particularly sad. At one conference I spoke at, I was seated at a table with (hold your breath) six Christian sexual therapists. Their reasoned opinion is that marital sex takes twenty years to reach its peak, at which point it can be more enjoyable than ever. To pursue this, however, you're going to have to grow as a couple in many areas that aren't easy to grow in. Keeping this aspect of marriage alive and fulfilling long-term is, in fact, one of the great challenges of marriage (but also one of the most thrilling; it is beyond wonderful to so desire someone you know so well and love so dearly and with whom you have so many pleasant memories).

The difficulty of maintaining long-term sexual interest can actually be a blessing. Achieving sexual satisfaction will all but force you to develop the same relational skills that will serve all aspects of marriage: you're going to have to be humble, to hear hard words, and to learn to put someone else's needs first; you're going to have to learn how to understand who your partner is and what he or she truly desires (and doesn't desire). You'll need plenty of courage, as it's easier to just stay quiet in this area than pursue true intimacy, to be as naked in your conversation and desires as you are in each other's arms. You will have to grow in empathy and patience and generosity.

That's why I believe it is a mark of God's kindness that it can be so difficult to maintain long-term sexual intimacy in marriage after the initial sexual chemistry has faded, because it forces us to develop the very skills needed for a marriage to succeed on all levels. If you grow in humility, if you learn how to listen, if you develop courage to bring something up instead of cowardly keeping silent, and if you create a marital climate where even the potentially embarrassing realities of "naked" life can be looked at under a microscope, there isn't an element of your marriage that won't benefit from these newly enhanced relational skills.

So is desire important for marital sexuality? Of course it is! But it's not just about discovering a new trick or a new position to keep desire alive; it's about building a relationship that feeds desire.

Lego Sets

Dr. Juli Slattery uses an analogy that I think is spot-on accurate. Long-term marital sexuality isn't like a Tonka truck; it's more like a Lego set. A Tonka truck comes out of the box ready to be played with. Kids can attack a mountain of dirt within seconds of taking the toy out of the box. But Legos are something entirely different: the fun is in putting something together. After you build something, however, it's not that much fun for very long. You might enjoy building a Lego boat, but who wants to play with a Lego boat for more than five minutes? So you tear it apart and rebuild something else.

In the same way, to maintain lifelong enjoyment sexually, we have to build, tear down, and rebuild our sexual relationships with our spouses. Sex is one thing when you're newlyweds and alone at home. It changes, though, after it becomes routine and you've gotten familiar with each other. There's another challenge altogether when kids enter the picture, including pregnancy and nursing and the exhaustion of having your sleep schedules blown up. It changes yet again when those kids become toddlers, and then teenagers, and then when your bodies begin to struggle with age.

In any one of these seasons it is easy to give up. If you've built a sex life that "worked" when you were newlyweds, it's not necessarily going to work with two toddlers and a baby at home. And it most likely would be a disaster when you hit your sixties. If you don't reinvent your sexual relationship, intentionally and purposefully, it's going to fade. The canary is going to die.

Let me get very "physical" in the next section. God created our bodies as well as our souls; when we understand how our bodies (including our brains) function, we can understand the role of desire and love in a sacred marriage.

Sexual Windows

It helps wives to understand that their husbands walk around with quite a bit less oxytocin, a neurochemical that creates feelings of warmth and affection, than they do. If a woman has a high level of oxytocin and the man she's married to has a below-average amount, the difference can be a factor of ten. There is one time in human experience, however, when a man's level of oxytocin—those neurochemicals that make him feel close to his wife and bonded with his wife—approaches that of a woman's. It's immediately following sexual climax.

Women, why do your husbands want to have sex with you as often as they do (whether they realize this or not)?* They may never feel closer to you than immediately following sexual consummation.

Remember—this is by God's design. Because wives already have more elevated levels of oxytocin, they may not notice the uptick after sex as much as men do. If you're already mostly full, eating a sandwich doesn't make you feel that much better.

Now, add to the absence of a man's oxytocin the presence of sexual hormones and the general effect of testosterone. This "stew" creates a situation such that when a man moves past what we could call his "sexual window," his sexual desire can become virtually an obsession. Breasts seem to appear out of nowhere, magnets to his eyes. He notices a pair of legs in a way he wouldn't have a day or two ago. A provocative advertisement yanks his attention with a force that can startle him. Testosterone creates a programmed lens that gives sexual meaning to the world.

Every man has a different sexual window, and these windows can certainly change with age. For your husband, the window might be twenty-four hours, three days, or a week. But if he's pushed past that window, and you're not available, sexual desire can feel like a freight train pulling him away from you and toward something—or someone—else.

---

* Certainly, many guys are driven by lust, not a desire to feel closer to their wives, but that's a different discussion. Let's focus here on God's creational intent.

When sexual desire is met in marriage, that window is wonderfully reset; lust will still be a battle for most men, but it's the difference between saying no to a dessert after having eaten a full meal and turning down a burger when you haven't eaten in three days. It's a different fight altogether.

And here's the payoff, for both of you: By meeting that desire, you release all kinds of very positive oxytocin in your husband's brain, and he rebonds with you all over again. He learns to trust you. He was vulnerable, and you didn't use that against him. He learns to treasure you. He needed you, and you were there for him. He learns to appreciate you. He has an intense desire that feels like it could rule him, but that desire dissipates in your arms, with an aftermath that feels like the Garden of Eden instead of a guilt-ridden jaunt through accusatory hell.

Going back to the men, let me say this: Our sexual desires will either bless our marriages or ruin our integrity. If we ignore them, pretend that they won't drive us, or that they can exist without healthy fulfillment, we're being foolish unless God has given us the gift of celibacy. I've sat across from too many men who felt overly confident about their ability to coast in sexless marriages—for a while. That while ended, tragically so, and that's why they're sitting in my office with weeping wives and shame written all over their faces.

God has given us such strong desires to keep our marriages together, not to tear them apart, so we need to be intentional about channeling our desires in the right direction. If your sexual relationship has crumbled, I'm calling on you as the husband to figure out why. That may mean finding out what you're doing (or not doing) outside the bedroom that's keeping your wife uninterested. It may mean paying a visit to the doctor, getting your wife some help with her job or household chores, or listening to something you're doing that is undercutting your appearance or desirability.

It may also mean being more intentional and thoughtful about meeting your wife's desires rather than focusing on your own.

The Depths of Desire

"Talk about world domination!"

My wife had been in a busy season, so I purposefully had planned an evening I knew she would enjoy—dinner at a jazz club followed by an evening of romance. I intentionally let the sexual energy smolder throughout the day. Well before dinnertime, Lisa finally suggested, "Why don't we just get on with it already?" but I simply smiled at her and thought, *Not a chance.*

On the way to the club, I filled up her car's gas tank because I know Lisa hates to fill up her gas tank and she was going to be driving the next day. That may not sound so sexually enticing, but it's not up to us men to determine what constitutes foreplay. Trust me, men—something like that can do wonders; it builds the mood. It makes your wife think, *He's taking care of me.* A spiritually healthy wife who feels taken care of is supernaturally predisposed to take care of you.

The "dinner" (iceberg lettuce masquerading as a salad, poorly cooked chicken covered with gravy, *instant* mashed potatoes) was a disaster given Lisa's organic bent, but she loved the music and atmosphere. It's not a place I would have gone to on my own— Lisa knew we were there because of her.

My small touches during the dinner were intentional and deliberate, but nothing scandalous. If someone from our church had been sitting right behind us, they wouldn't have even noticed; but I've been married to Lisa for twenty-nine years and pretty much know how, even in public, I can slowly bring her near to a boiling point with touches and caresses that no one watching could possibly take offense to or even know what was going on. After nearly three decades of enjoying each other, an innocent-looking caress, a simple touch, a slight moving of her hair can bring to mind past memories and a future promise that are packed with impending pleasure.

When we got home, I knew what I was going to do, and I did it. It wasn't anything grand, just intentional and thoughtful, and it showed a little preparation. Within minutes Lisa was lying back saying, "Talk about world domination!"

What she meant was "You have conquered me. Do what you will."

When it first came out, the *Fifty Shades of Grey* trilogy was discussed by more marital and Christian bloggers than could be counted, so let me just say this: men, if you need handcuffs and ropes to make your wife feel the enticement of full surrender, you might be doing it wrong.

Try studying her, getting to know her moods and total body— not just the most popular three areas of feminine anatomy, but everything.

Try kindness, on a daily basis.

Try spiritual connection—make sure she knows she's supported in prayer.

Try years of giving pleasure unselfishly so that she knows, once everything gets started, she's going to be carried away by your touches, not used by your demands.

Try taking care of her kids and taking care of her.

Try thinking about how you're going to exceed her expectations. It's stunning to think about how good we can make our wives feel—now compare that to how awful it is to leave them unsatisfied because we are focusing exclusively on our own pleasure.

If you study your wife and then apply all this, you'll come to a place where you never need handcuffs—what you've got is much stronger, more powerful, more exciting, and more fulfilling—a lifelong love of kept promises and generous service.

When our kids were young and at home, simply caring for them was much more effective than using handcuffs. When the kids were in rough spots and I took them out, or when they were starting to make some dubious choices and I sat down with them and talked with them and prayed with them, Lisa's natural response was, "You're such a good dad. And let me show you how a wife shows her appreciation for a man who loves her kids ..."

My wife's take is that women would be less inclined to read about sex with an imaginary billionaire if they were fully enjoying real sex with thoughtful husbands. She's not saying if a wife is reading erotic novels that her husband is a poor lover—just that it might be a symptom that things have started to slide in the bedroom. "I don't think most women want pain or the kind of sex described in those books," Lisa told me. "I just think they want something a little more creative than what they're getting."

Men, God has given us the capacity with our bodies to take our wives to places of transcendent pleasure. We can make our wives forget, for a few blessed moments, that they are moms who need to wipe noses and change diapers; they can forget that they are bosses with lazy employees, or employees with buffoon bosses; they can forget that there is a house to clean or a doctor's appointment to remember or a car to vacuum or a sick friend to call. They can be transported to a divine-like place of sighs and holy pleasure and laughter and delight, and when it's all done, we will feel closer to them than ever before.

Only God could make something like this happen.

The world's form of pleasure is almost always a cheap substitute of the real thing, and it's never as satisfying. I don't see how what I've heard depicted in *Fifty Shades* could possibly be sustained long-term. Building immediate desire at the cost of long-term intimacy might get you through the weekend, but it won't sustain your marriage through your kids' high school graduation.

And yet the immediacy of desire always pushes us toward short-term solutions, doesn't it? A guy can't get his wife excited, so he looks at porn to watch some other guy get a woman excited. A man can't get his wife to the place of appropriate surrender, so he resorts to silly things like handcuffs and ropes and not-so-silly things like pain to bring a little "spice" into the bedroom.

I'm not into constructing Christian lists of dos and don'ts. I don't want to marginalize something that you and your wife have enjoyed, so please don't take this the wrong way. I'm just saying that long-term sexual satisfaction in marriage has to go well beyond gimmicks. If you want to use a gimmick now and then, fine—it's your marriage. But if you think something like that is going to sustain you through the years, you're fooling yourself.

For long-term satisfaction, study your wife, not just a few parts of her body. Build years of trust with kind touching and generous pleasuring. Let her know that if she lets herself go in your hands you'll make her momentarily forget everything bad going on in her life and feel everything good. If you can't get her excited in public, fully clothed, if you need to get her "naked and handcuffed" to feel like things are getting hot, you probably don't know her well enough yet.

And, guys, it's perfectly holy and God honoring to think about how to sexually please and thrill your wife. God knows His daughters work hard and live in a world that neglects them; do you think He has a problem with us cherishing them, desiring them (and healing their souls in the process), and then releasing in them what God designed for their good—a supremely enjoyable climax?

Not a chance. Frankly, I'm of the opinion that God likely wishes we'd have far more sex, not less.

It is godly to surrender to the desire of marital sex. Far better to fantasize about ways to take your wife to a new place of pleasure than to spend one second fantasizing about any other woman.

So, to summarize all this, yes, desire matters, particularly in the bedroom. It's celebrated in the Song of Songs. If you haven't had moments in your marriage when you were burning with passion for your spouse, I feel sorry for you. It's a wonderful experience to know everything you want is right there waiting for you, with guaranteed fulfillment. No tricks, no lies, no empty promises— what a blessing to have a desire that can be fulfilled in such a fun, pleasurable, and holy way.

But what will create and sustain such desire through the years, given the fact that we are sinful people married to other sinful people? *Everything we've talked about in this book.* Literally every chapter, once it's applied, can serve your sex life.

In the previous chapter we defined true love as a "shared experience of God living in us and God's love being made complete in us." Sex showcases this; it doesn't compete with it. There's a reason so many commentators used to read the Song of Songs as a type of our passionate desire for God.

Desire isn't a problem; properly focused, it's a blessing. But a lifelong love doesn't exist on desire alone; it's the other way around. Love sustains the desire; desire doesn't sustain the love. If I truly love my wife outside the bedroom, I will crave her touch between the sheets and she will crave mine. If I must desire before I love, my sexuality and my attitudes will be as spotty as the weather— hot one day and cold the next.

Building a Lifelong Love

1. What does this chapter say about the importance of cultivating and sustaining long-term sexual intimacy?
2. Has your sexual relationship with each other brought more healing than hurt? Why do you think that is so? What do you need to do to grow as a couple in this area in the future?
3. Talk with your spouse about one or two times when you felt the pleasure of sexual intimacy with each other at its most intense. What was happening? What set it up? What does this tell you about your relationship and how to build desire in the future?
4. Wives, do you know what your husbands' sexual windows are? Men, be honest in sharing with your wives about how long you can go without sex before it feels like it's becoming an obsession.
5. Wives, be bold and tell your husbands what will most serve you sexually. Give your husbands something to shoot for! It's healthy for them to focus on this, and you will likely receive a nice payoff.

Our creator God, You who have designed our bodies and brains, who has called us together as husband and wife, let the two of us boldly claim the intimacy of sexual pleasure. Give us courage to be honest with each other and to reach new levels of intimacy outside the bedroom so that we can reach new levels of pleasure and fulfillment inside the bedroom. Grant us servants' hearts and clear consciences to plumb the depths of marital love. In Jesus's name, amen.

21

Living Is Giving

A man who heard me speak on marriage decided to apply my suggestion that men use every act of sexual temptation as an opportunity to actively do something for their wives. One of the best ways for husbands to fight lust for other women is to be consumed with loving their wives. We go much further focusing on loving extravagantly than on not falling. So, very practically, we use temptation as a reminder to pay attention to our marriages rather than to indulge the possibility of stepping into sin.

In this case, the advice served the man well. He arrived home from work earlier than usual, and his wife was gone. Normally, this would have been a time when the temptation to look at pornography became intense.

Remembering what I had said, he decided to take on a chore that his wife normally did: he mowed the lawn.

When his wife got home and saw him putting away the lawn mower, she was shocked. "What's going on?" she asked.

"Nothing. I just got home early and saw that the lawn hadn't been mowed, figured you were busy, and thought I'd help you out."

She hugged him like she meant it—for maybe the first time in weeks.

"I can't believe how much difference it made just doing that one simple thing," he said.

Sometimes, people talk about "giving up sin," as if doing so is a loss. I like to talk about the *cost* of sin, what it takes away from us. Most of us are busy. When we cultivate any sin that consumes our time, something else has to die, and it's usually the good things that do. Opportunities are lost and relationships are neglected. Even more, sin turns us inward and we lose the thrilling joy that comes from a life focused on giving.

Have you ever asked yourself what your sin is keeping you from? What is it costing you? Instead of focusing simply on not doing that sin, why not use temptation as a reminder to perform an act of love? Do someone's chore. Write a letter of encouragement. Pick out an unexpected present. Send an email or text to someone you love.

All of this teaching is based on my understanding that we can actually use temptation to become more like Christ. This might sound crazy, but not if we understand that for the Christian, *to live is to give*. And if temptation reminds me to give, I can use it instead of being blown apart by it.

The most telling transformation of a true disciple is that we are turned from selfish people who live for pleasure and our own comfort into disciples who are dedicated to serving others: "Though I am free and belong to no one, I have made myself a slave to everyone, to win as many as possible" (1 Cor. 9:19).

The mark of Jesus is the mark of a giver. His greatest love is seen in giving His life for others, a love of which Jesus said there is none greater (John 15:13).

If Jesus truly lives in us, we can't help but give. We are eager to give. We delight in giving. We look for opportunities to give. And we should never get tired of giving: "Let us not become weary in doing good, for at the proper time we will reap a harvest if we do not give up. Therefore, as we have opportunity, let us do good to all people, especially to those who belong to the family of believers" (Gal. 6:9–10).

Two women wrote a remarkable daily devotional that became a huge bestseller in the early half of the twentieth century. In *God Calling* they sensed God telling them, "Give abundantly. Feel that you are rich. Have no mean thought in your heart. Of Love, of thought, of all you have, give, give, give. You are followers of the World's Greatest Giver. Give of time, of personal ease and comfort, of rest, of fame, of healing, of power, of sympathy, of all these and many more. Learn this lesson, and you will become a great power to help others and to do mighty things."[1]

Give, give, give …

Brothers and sisters, is there any calling in life that teaches us to give, give, give quite like marriage and parenting? This is a training ground for what it means to be ruled by our Lord

Jesus, the chief Giver, who gives us His Holy Spirit, who compels and empowers us to give without limit.

Think of your selfishness like wet, dirty clothes. When you're tired, it's miserable taking the clothes off—pulling the wet shirt over your head, sliding the pants down, trying not to get dirt everywhere. It would be so much easier to just sit in them. But think how amazingly wonderful it feels when you get those clothes off, take a shower, and put on something fresh.

Heaven itself!

We've got to peel off our selfishness. It's filthy and wet and will make us sick. It's easiest just to sit in it, but God wants us to peel it off and be washed and clothed in His Holy Spirit, His *giving* Spirit. Some people talk of holiness as a burden to marriage—holiness is a burden to marriage as laughter is a burden to conversation or a loving caress is a burden to skin.

Jesus Himself promised us that it is better to give than to receive (Acts 20:35). That's *truth*. In Jesus's economy, giving is better than receiving. So what's with the complaints that you do all the giving and rarely get to receive? According to Jesus, you have a spectacular arrangement! You are laying aside huge heavenly rewards, you are growing by miles and miles, and your poor spouse is just sitting in those cold, damp, filthy clothes. You should feel sorry for him or her, not for yourself!

Or do you not believe that Jesus speaks the truth?

Will you let God use your family to help you cherish giving? Will you embrace a life of giving? Will you even thank Him for providing an arena in which you can give so abundantly?

Do Not Withhold Good

Many of us like to define our excellence as spouses by what we *don't* do: I don't get rough with my spouse, I don't gossip about my spouse, I don't yell at my spouse, I don't cheat on my spouse. But Proverbs 3:27 takes it to a new level, telling us that excellence is found in what we *do* do, not just what we avoid.

Listen to this: "Do not withhold good from those to whom it is due, when it is in your power to act." If you have the opportunity to bless your spouse while possessing the ability to do it, but out of laziness or malice or selfishness, you choose not to act, you're in direct violation of this teaching. It views sin as "withholding" rather than just "committing."

If my wife needs to talk and I have the power to talk but fail to do it, according to Proverbs 3:27, that's a problem. If I know my spouse needs to be encouraged but I'm too busy to notice or too apathetic to find a creative way to build her up, that's a problem. If my spouse thinks our sexual relationship is running on fumes and I can't marshal the energy to revitalize it, that's a problem. If our finances are causing my spouse tremendous stress and I don't step in to better manage it, by increasing income and/or curtailing expenses, I'm going against Scripture.

Instead of saying, "I'm an excellent spouse because I don't do x, y, or z," how about going a step further and saying, "Because I want to be an excellent spouse, today I'm going to do a, b, and c"?

What good are you able to do for your spouse or your kids but you aren't doing it for whatever reason? It doesn't have to be something that would necessarily qualify as a sin of omission if you didn't do it (not feeding your kids, never talking to your spouse are obvious sins). Think a little deeper about things that you know would bless your spouse or family, that you have the power to do, but for whatever reason—laziness, apathy, busyness—you're not doing them. Adopt a giving view of marriage. The "fantastic five" will help us do that.

The Fantastic Five

There must be something about the number five. Gary Chapman came up with *The Five Love Languages*, a book that's been on the bestseller list for so long that it must be growing moss. Shaunti Feldhahn more recently wrote the bestselling *The Surprising Secrets of Highly Happy Marriages*. Both books contain a wealth of information about how to love our spouses.

The challenge is that Gary Chapman and Shaunti Feldhahn took two entire books to help adequately equip us to love. What am I supposed to do in half a chapter? Well, for starters, I could tell you to pick up either or both books as a follow-up, but most of you have probably already read them anyway, so let me just summarize them very briefly right here. Of course, we all know that every spouse is different; we have to study our spouses to find out what they want to receive. Even if 99 percent of spouses respond in a certain way, that doesn't mean much if our spouses respond in a different way.

Gary Chapman talked about now well-known categories: words of affirmation, quality time, receiving gifts, acts of service, and physical touch. He offered explanations and suggestions for how we love our spouses in these ways.

Shaunti came up with her "fantastic five" for men and women through research. Most men agreed that these five things make them feel loved in marriage:

1. Noticing his effort and sincerely thanking him for it.
2. Verbally saying, "You did a great job at _____."
3. Praising him in front of others.
4. Demonstrating that you desire him sexually and that he pleases you sexually.
5. Making sure he knows that he makes you happy.

The "fantastic five" for women are:

1. Hold her hand.
2. Leave her a message (voice, text, email) that you're thinking about her.
3. Put your arm around her, touch her in the small of her back when you're walking, put your hand on her knee in public places.
4. Tell her, "You are beautiful."
5. When you're grumpy or depressed, get over it or talk about it, but don't withdraw.

Notice, please, that these are all active elements. They are all gifts. They all assume initiating. They all agree with Jesus's premise that living is giving.

If you want to be happy in your marriage, you have to be a giver. If you want your spouse to be happy in your marriage, you have to be a giver. It's safe to say that, thanks in part to Christian publishers, couples who truly care about this have more resources and tools and general knowledge to accomplish this aim than any generation of believers that has ever come before us. We can truly excel in love and, according to Shaunti, excel in happiness when we do this.

Slow and Steady, Not Big and Sweaty

My friend Kevin Harney was at a Promise Keepers conference years ago when the speaker asked every man to make a commitment to love his wife in a very practical way when he got home. Some men stood up and said they were going to wash their wives' cars. Another said he'd be sure to pick up his socks. One said he'd finally get around to installing some new program on his wife's computer.

Kevin prayed before he answered (always a dangerous thing to do), and he sensed God asking him, "What does Sherry hate doing the most?"

That was easy: making the bed.

Fine, Kevin thought, *when I get home, I'll make the bed for the next five days.*

"That's not what I meant," God seemed to reply. "Why not do it *every* day, and when you do it, pray for her?"

God was asking Kevin to make a lifetime commitment, which Kevin has kept, by the way. In fact, he did the math recently and found out that he is now approaching six thousand times of making the bed while praying for his wife. He even does this when he's at a hotel because he doesn't want to miss the chance to pray for his wife.

Intimate marriage isn't built on the big moments: an over-the-top proposal or hitting it out of the park on a birthday or anniversary. Those can be fun times, but the divorce court is littered with marriages that enjoyed occasional parties amid a wasteland of otherwise persistent apathy.

To truly grow our love, it's better to start small and be consistent rather than try to rescue things with a grand gesture. When you notice a malaise seeping into your marriage, or your partner makes you notice it with a theatrical display of discontent, it's tempting to think you can fix things with one big act of repentance. The problem is, you can't keep a grand gesture going. Its sweetness fades the further you get from it, making it ring hollow. It even sets up a false expectation: "See, he or she *can* do something nice." Ironically, it can even make things worse, for when it doesn't keep happening, it serves only to highlight the emptiness before and after.

One of the things I particularly like about Shaunti's teaching is that it captures this notion of doing small things consistently. A small act of kindness, repeated daily, will take you much further than a surprising onetime act of generosity. For instance, men, if your wife says, "You never notice me" so you take her out to dinner, write out a card with fifty things you appreciate about her, and buy her an extravagant gift, she'll feel appreciated for a few hours. If you go right back to where you were, thinking you've taken care of the problem, you'll actually be worse off seventy-two hours later. She'll resent that you seemed to "get it" but now are deliberately not getting it anymore. On the other hand, if you decide that you'll take some time to notice your wife for fifty days in a row, mentioning one new thing each day and perhaps following up with a small gesture of kindness four or five days a week, you'll go much further with your wife than a onetime event could ever accomplish. It will also produce a change within yourself that a single grand gesture could not.

Women, if your husband seems starved for sexual affection and you think one special night in a hotel where you plan, primp, and surprise him with your initiative will satisfy him for a while, you're sadly mistaken. All that will do is increase his appetite and make him want it more, which will make him miss its absence more. Far better to be consistent in showing sexual love two or three times a week than to think one grand gesture will make things better.

Marriage is about cultivating your character—not just your individual character, but also the character of your relationship. Character is grown out of small, consistent choices. Choosing to practice kindness, choosing to listen, and choosing to pray together turn us into kinder, humbler, more spiritually intimate people and couples. Grand gestures just whet the appetite for more; they don't usually satisfy the soul.

Small and steady will get you much further than "big and sweaty" or stupendous and rare. Choose something you can do— and keep on doing it.

You Had Me at Jell-O

My friends Paul and Virginia Friesen watched a friend's thirty-eight-year-old marriage come to a sad and painful end due to cancer. It was heartbreaking, and Wendy was devastated when she had to say a final good-bye to her husband.

By Wendy's own description, she and John had shared a "sweet marriage." Part of that sweet marriage involved flying to Hawaii twice each year; the islands held many special memories of their life together. For her first time back to Hawaii without John, Wendy asked Paul and Virginia to come along. She just couldn't bear to be alone, not this first time.

As the three of them shared a lunch out on the balcony over-looking the Pacific, Wendy started to cry.

"What is it, Wendy?" Paul asked.

To his surprise, she blurted out, "I wish I'd made him more Jell-O!"

Jell-O? Her husband's gone and she's thinking about *Jell-O?*

I'll let Paul and Virginia explain the rest:

"Wendy then told us, through laughter and tears, that John loved Jell-O. From the earliest days of their marriage, John always was asking her to make him Jell-O. She didn't like Jell-O herself and declined to make it most of the time, claiming it was all empty calories, nothing but sugar and colored dyes. But now, looking back, she mused, 'Why didn't I just give him Jell-O?' As we continued to talk, she said, 'The real reason was not all the nutritional stuff, but just that I plain didn't want to make him Jell-O. I didn't like it. But what a simple thing for me to do to bring him a little extra joy for the day. I wish I had made him more Jell-O.'"

When you look back on your marriage, what will be your "Jell-O," that silly little thing that you denied giving to your spouse? Paul and Virginia presented some piercing comments: "It is my deep conviction that we truly are designed to be at our best when we put our spouse's needs above our own. The irony is that when we do, we actually find the intimacy we have been longing for.... Just as Wendy wished she'd made John more Jell-O, at some point in life, each of us will look back and reflect on our marriage and what could have made it more what we desired and what God designed it to be."[2]

What will it be? What's your spouse's "Jell-O"?

Secret Service

One final thought in this regard is the biblical notion of doing our deeds in secret. Marriage must have obvious acts of love and service and giving, of course, but I believe a truly sacred marriage, with a spouse's hope set on the judgment day, will also have many moments of "secret service" in which we do things for our spouses that they will not recognize or even know about.

As a spiritual exercise, this is win-win-win-win. My spouse is served (win #1), and my lust to be noticed and appreciated is crucified (win #2) so that I can grow in the art of true, unselfish love (win #3). Furthermore, Jesus says it is when our works are done in secret that we can expect heavenly rewards (win #4).

This can be fun and worshipful and so beneficial. Take a few moments—consider right now how you can love your spouse by an act of secret service.

Building a Lifelong Love

1. What is your greatest temptation in life right now? Is there any way that serving your spouse in the face of that temptation (rather than indulging in the sin) can help you overcome that temptation?

2. In this chapter we read Proverbs 3:27: "Do not withhold good from those to whom it is due, when it is in your power to act." Is there any good you are withholding from your spouse?

3. This will take a bit more work, but it's worth it: Write out your own "fantastic five," the five small, consistent things your spouse can do to make you feel especially loved. Now, write out what you think your spouse's fantastic five would be (you can use Shaunti's list as a starting point). Next, exchange lists on a date night and talk about growing in your love for each other.

4. What small, daily act (such as Kevin Harney making the bed and praying for his wife) can you begin doing to adopt a "living is giving" mind-set?

5. Pray about a "secret service" you can do in the next month to love your spouse, in a way that only God will know what you have done.

God of truth, give us minds that believe You when You say that it is better to give than to receive. Every selfish fiber in our beings makes us think otherwise. We've read Your truth; now please convict us of Your truth. Let us be transformed by the renewing of our minds so that we can become extravagant givers. Please give us understanding of each other's needs and desires; help us to find those small actions that will encourage and support them, and then please give us hearts as generous as Yours so that we will eagerly perform those actions. In Jesus's name, amen.

Epilogue

If you looked up "lifelong love" in a sermon illustration dictionary, you'd likely find a picture of Jim and Anne Pierson. This couple has been my Halley's Comet for much of my adult life, passing by every few years. I met them in my twenties while working at Care Net; they ran their own ministry with a similar emphasis named Loving and Caring. We'd see each other at conferences and conventions and catch up on each other's lives and ministries. They saw my children grow up and my hair fall out.

When I left Care Net in my thirties to focus on writing and speaking, I was still invited to the conferences, and Jim was a shelter to me. I'm an insecure introvert, called to an extrovert's job, and Jim was a solid place of refuge between sessions. Anne was always such an encouraging presence; she believed in me. She spoke so passionately of how God was using me, in a way I had to believe her, even in the face of my insecurities. Having done for more than a decade what I had just started doing, Anne was a wonderful role model.

Jim was a giant of a man; I'm guessing if the scale didn't reach 350 to 400 pounds, it wouldn't be of much use to him. His large girth carried an even larger heart, as he was a dad, pastor, counselor, and mentor to so many people. Though he could be hilarious (I once saw him hold up a hotel-sized bath soap in front of his belly and ask an entire room, "So, they think this is going to be enough?"), Jim usually worked behind the scenes. Anne was the teacher, the speaker, and the trainer. Jim ran their book table and kept Anne's life on track.

There was a time when Jim would steal the spotlight, however. Before every one of Anne's workshops, just after she was introduced, Jim would slip into the back of the room and belt out the Stevie Wonder tune, "Isn't she lovely? Isn't she wonderful?"

The largely feminine audience ate this up, to see a husband affirm his wife so well.

Sadly, Jim had a long and difficult death. He contracted an unusual form of aggressive cancer that, when diagnosed, doctors said would send him home to the Lord within a couple of weeks. Jim hung on for seven months, but they were brutal months sprinkled with some incredible times of ministry. So many people had to cycle through his hospice room to say good-bye that Anne thinks Jim was holding on for their sakes.

The medical costs associated with his end-of-life care would have bankrupted Jim's family if not for the aid of a wealthy business-man whom Jim had led to the Lord. Jim had discipled this man via telephone on a weekly basis for years.

"He made me a much better man, a much better father, a much better husband. I want to cover the costs of his care, Anne."

"I don't think you realize how much this is going to cost," Anne protested.

"I don't think you realize how much of an impact Jim has had on my life," the man responded. "Please, let me do this for him."

After Jim finally died, Anne went to her next conference with a heavy heart. Jim had always been there for her, and she had to brace herself to be introduced and not hear Jim break out with his Stevie Wonder song.

Sure enough, the introduction ended, Anne looked up, felt enveloped by the silence, and then apologized. "I'm sorry," she told the crowd, "I just need to pray."

She bowed her head to find strength in God, and when she opened her eyes, someone had placed a flower in a vase right in front of her. Anne was startled, thrown off.

"What's this?" she asked the crowd.

A woman in the front row explained that she had woken up that morning and felt impressed by God that Anne would need something encouraging right before she started speaking. She told her husband to go get a flower in a vase.

"Where am I going to find that?" he asked. "We're not from around here."

"*Just get it,*" she said.

So he did. Anne then told the gathered audience about how Jim had always sung to her before she spoke, how she had dreaded opening her eyes and hearing nothing, and how much that flower meant to her, evidence that God was still with her even though her husband wasn't and God would see her through.

As you might expect, there was a serious run on Kleenex in that room. And the husband, who admitted that he had protested his wife's request rather vigorously, told Anne, "I'm going to be a different husband. I had no idea how much those small things can really matter."

Jim had discipled another man *in his death*.

The first time I saw Anne after Jim's passing, I was fighting back tears approximately every fifteen minutes as we remembered her wonderful husband. As she dropped me off at my hotel, she paused to tell me, "I've had such a good life, Gary. Such a good, good life, investing in others and sharing that with Jim."

Though people always spoke so highly of the gifted Anne Pierson, for every one time I heard her name in ministry circles I heard "Jim and Anne Pierson" a dozen times. They had that blessed single identity. They were a unit—two individuals who were very much a single couple.

Jim and Anne had little of what most people think constitutes a glamorous marriage. Having spent their entire married lives in ministry, they had so little money that Jim felt he needed to get permission from Anne to leave his daughter a small gift in his will (less than $10,000) to buy a new car. They didn't look like Angelina Jolie and Brad Pitt. Jim's passing was covered by a local newspaper, but it didn't make the evening news or even *Christianity Today*. But how many people do you know who can look back at a simple but spiritually fruitful life and honestly say, "It's been such a good life, Gary. Such a good, good life, investing in others and sharing that with my husband"?

You don't have to be beautiful (though Jim and Anne are, in every way). You don't have to be rich. You don't have to be famous to experience this. You just have to be what Jim and Anne were: worshippers of God, intent on seeking *first* His kingdom and His righteousness, investing in the lives of others, and reaping eternal rewards.

God wants this for you. He wants you to say good-bye to your lifelong love with similar words, "It has been such a good, good life, a rich life of investing in others and sharing that with my spouse."

We began with Jeremiah 31, so let's end there. After God said through Jeremiah, "I have loved you with an everlasting love; therefore I have drawn you with lovingkindness. Again I will build you and you will be rebuilt" (vv. 3–4 NASB), He added, "I will make them walk by streams of waters, on a straight path in which they will not stumble; for I am a father to Israel" (v. 9 NASB).

God will make us walk; God will lead us on a "straight path" and keep us from stumbling. Why? He is our Father and, once we are married, also our Father-in-Law.

"'They will come and shout for joy on the height of Zion, and they will be radiant over the bounty of the LORD.... Their life will be like a watered garden ... For I will turn their mourning into joy and will comfort them and give them joy for their sorrow.... *My people will be satisfied with My goodness*,' declares the LORD" (vv. 12–14 NASB).

Holiness is the guardian of happiness, not its enemy. If you live a life of holiness in your marriage, you will be more than satisfied with God's goodness.

Anne looked at me behind glasses with eyes that had seen many decades, but those were satisfied eyes, eyes convinced of God's goodness, grateful for every day.

Married life, offered in service to God, is such a good and rewarding life. Let's give ourselves fully to it; let's keep building our "marital house" until we die, pursuing each other, forgiving each other, loving each other, and growing together through the years. If we do this, we will, like Anne, be richly blessed with a lifelong love.

Appendix

God Hates Domestic Violence

Two days before Christmas, I accidentally sent a decorative reindeer hurtling off a small table in our library. This reindeer shattered into five separate pieces. I picked up each piece, knowing there was no way I could repair this, and presented the evidence to Lisa.

"That's fine," she said, surprising me. "It wasn't that expensive, and I wasn't that into it."

Our passion over the destruction of something is directly related to how important it is to us. On another occasion, I dropped a glass cup that had belonged to Lisa's grandmother. The cup was precious to her. Lisa didn't even have to speak. I could feel the passion.

When will we men understand how precious God's daughters—our wives—are to Him? That to hurt them, to even make them miserable, raises a passion that we can't even imagine? If we don't strive to understand the depths of God's love for our wives, we'll miss the breadth of His wrath when we abuse them. "Since you call on a Father who judges each person's work impartially, live out your time as foreigners here in reverent fear" (1 Pet. 1:17).

The force of a sacred marriage—love, absolute benevolence, living to bless each other and showcase each other, being for the other, nurturing each other, encouraging each other—is diametrically opposed to any form of assault. The church should hate domestic violence as much as it hates divorce. When we assume that God hates divorce more than He hates domestic violence, it shows how little we understand His passion for His daughters. It also leads to the disastrous consequence of making women feel like they are obligated to stay in a dangerous situation that God hates. The last thing a woman fleeing a dangerous home should feel is guilt. She is serving God's purpose by ending something He hates—violence against her.

Dallas Willard rightfully broadened the definition of *assault* to other forms of violence that may not be physical: "Merely avoiding domestic violence can still leave the home a hell of cutting remarks, contempt, coldness, and withdrawal or noninvolvement. Such a hell is often found in the homes of Christians and even of Christian leaders."[1] Not all forms of such activity may warrant divorce, but they certainly raise the wrath of God and deserve to be called out every bit as much as God's hatred of divorce.

Pastors, we must hold all forms of marital assault with the same contempt with which God holds it. Sometimes, it seems like we are more concerned with keeping the marriage going than ending the violence, when in reality, violent men need to understand that in order to keep the marriage going, the violence must stop, *now*. Notice how we put the onus on the woman instead of the man: "Wife, stay in the marriage" rather than "Husband, we cannot support your wife staying with you as long as you harm her."

We won't counsel like this until we hate domestic violence as much as God hates it. The harm it does to the children; the deplorable witness it gives to the world; the damage it does to a woman's soul (not to mention her body); the corrupting influence it has on the male perpetrator; the pain it causes our heavenly Father-in-Law who hates to see His daughters abused—it is as ugly a sin as you can find.

Would you ever counsel your daughter to stay in a place where she winces when she sees a knife or flinches when her husband touches her? Would you ever tell her to spend a night in a home where she's not entirely sure she'll wake up alive or unbruised in the morning? Wouldn't you do everything in your power to get her out of there, sooner rather than later?

. Every Christian wife should be able to look at her husband's hands not as a threat but as a source of provision—he will work hard for her and her children. She should view his hands not as instruments of pain but as tools of tremendous sexual pleasure—over the course of their marriage, he should provide countless sessions of loving caresses and experienced affection. His hands should be thought of as a source of protection—those hands will become a fist only to protect the family he loves, never, not even once, to turn on them.

When we think keeping a marriage together is the only biblical solution, even if it means preserving a violent situation, we have become beholders of legalism and strangers to God's true passion. The destruction of a marriage is a terrible thing; the destruction of a woman's soul, the damage to the children's psyches, and the triumph of fear and hatred where there should be faith, hope, and love are just as bad.

The last thing I am is "soft" on divorce. I have pleaded with couples to reconcile, and I have stressed that making a poor choice in your twenties doesn't give you an escape clause in your thirties when you meet a "better" choice.

But when I truly understand that my wife is God's daughter—that every believing woman is God's daughter—domestic violence isn't something I just want to "treat." It's something I've learned to hate, as God hates it. And if getting the woman out of the house is the only way to bring it to an end, then the sin is on the man who hurts, not the woman who flees.

When Jesus seemed so hard and so cold to the scribes, when He called them out and sounded nothing less than vicious in His denunciations, what was He angry about? "They that devour widows' houses" (Mark 12:40 ASV).

If we start messing with God's daughters, we're hitting Him where it hurts the most. We're raising the most furious of His passions. We're putting ourselves directly in the line of His red-hot wrath.

My friend Dr. Steve Wilke's contention that marital abuse is "any non-nurturing behavior" may not be the standard for divorce, but it is most definitely the benchmark of every sacred marriage.

I have been told that my book *Sacred Marriage* has been used as an argument for abused women to grit their teeth and bear it. The only one more appalled by this than me is God. I want to leave no misunderstanding about where I stand in this book, and thus offer this appendix to make it absolutely clear that any form of marital abuse, especially domestic violence, is in direct violation of a lifelong love. It goes against the spirit of every chapter of this book that I offer before God, to you.

Author Information

Feel free to contact Gary at gary@garythomas.com. Though he cannot respond personally to all correspondence, he welcomes your feedback. Please understand, however, that he is neither qualified nor able to provide counsel via email.

For information about Gary's speaking schedule, visit his website: www.garythomas.com. You can follow Gary on Twitter (@garyLthomas) or on Facebook (www.facebook.com /authorgarythomas). To inquire about inviting Gary to your church or community, visit his website and click on "Contact."

We especially invite you to visit Gary's blog, which focuses on married life (though many posts are written for singles who want to get married): www.garythomas.com/blog.

Notes

Chapter 1: The Magnificent Obsession

1. Jonathan Edwards, *The Works of Jonathan Edwards*, vol. 2, rev. Edward Hickman (London: Ball, Arnold, and Co., 1840), 5.

2. Gary Thomas, *Sacred Marriage: What If God Designed Marriage to Make Us Holy More Than to Make Us Happy?* (Grand Rapids, MI: Zondervan, 2000).

Chapter 2: Worshipping Our Way to Happiness

1. Annejet Campbell, comp., *Listen for a Change* (London: Grosvenor, 1986), 90, 93.

Chapter 3: Making the Last Things the First Thing Today

1. Jonathan Edwards, "The Christian Pilgrim," in *The Protestant Pulpit: An Anthology of Master Sermons from the Reformation to Our Own Day*, comp. Andrew W. Blackwood (Grand Rapids, MI: Baker, 1977), 41.

2. Edwards, *Protestant Pulpit*, 41.

3. Edwards, *Protestant Pulpit*, 44.

4. Edwards, *Protestant Pulpit*, 48.

Chapter 4: The Glory of Spiritual Dependence

1. John Milton, as cited in Harold Cooke Phillips, "An Angel in the Sun," in *The Protestant Pulpit: An Anthology of Master Sermons from the Reformation to Our Own Day*, comp. Andrew W. Blackwood (Grand Rapids, MI: Baker, 1977), 254.

2. Rob Rienow and Amy Rienow, *Visionary Marriage: Capture a God-Sized Vision for Your Marriage* (Nashville: Randall, 2010), 19–20.

3. C. H. Spurgeon, *Lectures to My Students, Complete and Unabridged* (Grand Rapids, MI: Zondervan, 1954), 96.

Chapter 5: Got Mission?

1. Kevin Miller and Karen Miller, *More Than You and Me: Touching Others Through the Strength of Your Marriage* (Colorado Springs: Focus on the Family, 1994), 3.

2. Miller and Miller, *More Than You and Me*, 6.

3. Miller and Miller, *More Than You and Me*, 7.

4. Miller and Miller, *More Than You and Me*, 8.

5. Julie Hatsell Wales, "Letters," *Marriage Partnership*, Winter 1991, 8.

6. Miller and Miller, *More Than You and Me*, introduction.

Chapter 8: Do Your Duty: The Surprising Call to Happiness

1. John Chrysostom, *On Marriage and Family Life*, trans. Catherine Roth and David Anderson (Crestwood, NY: St. Vladimir's Seminary, 1986), 54.

Part 2 (Growing Together)

1. Horace Bushnell, "Every Man's Life a Plan of God," in *The Protestant Pulpit: An Anthology of Master Sermons from the Reformation to Our Own Day*, comp. Andrew W. Blackwood (Grand Rapids, MI: Baker, 1977), 80.

Chapter 9: Supernatural Science

1. Lauren Fleshman, "To Heck with Science," *Runner's World*, September 2013, 56–57.

2. Calum MacLeod, "China Puts Up Roadblocks for Car Collectors," *USA Today*, October 23, 2013, 10A.

Chapter 11: Pushing Past the Power Shifts

1. Kayt Sukel, *This Is Your Brain on Sex: The Science Behind the Search for Love* (New York: Simon & Schuster, 2012), 5.

2. Kim Painter, "Moms Really *Do* Have a Nose for That Baby Smell," *USA Today*, October 2, 2013, 5D.

3. Annejet Campbell, comp., *Listen for a Change* (London: Grosvenor, 1986), 4.

4. The quotes in this section are taken from three sources: a personal lecture and subsequent private conversation with Dr. Robertson McQuilkin; and Robertson McQuilkin, *A Promise Kept: The Story of an Unforgettable Love* (Carol Stream, IL: Tyndale, 1998), 3, 13, 18–19, 22, 31–33, 50–53.

Chapter 13: The Two Dimensions of Marriage

1. John Chrysostom, *On Marriage and Family Life*, trans. Catherine Roth and David Anderson (Crestwood, NY: St. Vladimir's Seminary, 1986), 62.

Chapter 15: How One Couple Rescued a "Love Lost" Marriage

1. Gary Thomas, "Slowly Putting It Back Together: How One Couple Rescued a 'Love Lost' Marriage," *Gary Thomas* (blog), September 25, 2013, http://www.garythomas.com/rescued-a-lost-love-marriage/.

Chapter 16: Our Greatest Need

1. Linda Dillow, *What's It Like to Be Married to Me?* (Colorado Springs: David C Cook, 2011), 111–13.

Chapter 17: Absolute Benevolence

1. The essay was published posthumously. See "The Essence of True Virtue" in *The Works of President Edwards*, vol. 3, ed. S. E. Dwight (New York: S. Converse, 1829), 93–100; or "The Nature of True Virtue" in *Jonathan Edwards: Basic Writings*, ed. Ola Winslow (New York: Signet Classic Books, 1966), 241–49.

Chapter 19: Love Isn't Desire

1. Dallas Willard, *Renovation of the Heart: Putting on the Character of Christ* (Colorado Springs: NavPress, 2002), 132.

Chapter 21: Living Is Giving

1. A. J. Russell, ed., *God Calling*, expanded ed. (Uhrichsville, OH: Barbour, 2011), August 30 entry.

2. Paul Friesen and Virginia Friesen, *The Marriage App: Unlocking the Irony of Intimacy* (Bedford, MA: Home Improvement Ministries, 2013), 21–22, 167.

Appendix: God Hates Domestic Violence

1. Dallas Willard, *Renovation of the Heart: Putting on the Character of Christ* (Colorado Springs: NavPress, 2002), 190.

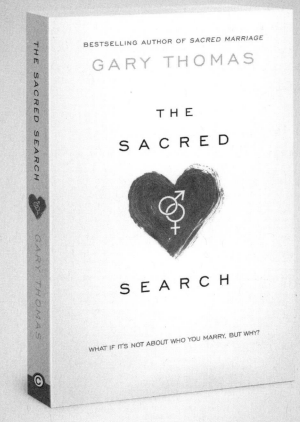